MASTERMIND
Jerry Moffatt

First published in 2017 by Café Kraft GmbH.
This edition first published in 2022 by Vertebrate Publishing.

VERTEBRATE PUBLISHING
Omega Court, 352 Cemetery Road, Sheffield S11 8FT, United Kingdom.
www.adventurebooks.com

Mastermind first edition editorial:
Producer and art direction: Hannes Huch
Layout, graphic design and illustrations: Marion Hett
Translation: Flo Scheimpflug
Editing: Simon Moffatt

Vertebrate Publishing is committed to printing on paper from sustainable sources.

MIX
Paper from
responsible sources
FSC® C014138
www.fsc.org

Printed and bound in Europe by Latitude Press.

NAME:

START DATE:

 MY GOALS:

MY SUCCESSES:

FOREWORD

When I was a young climber in the early 1990s, Jerry inspired me in so many ways. His boulder problem in Yosemite, *Dominator*, was the standard by which everything else was measured, and it opened my eyes to how cool bouldering is and the level of difficulty that can be achieved in just a few moves.

I remember bouldering in Camp 4 with Ron Kauk, the king of footwork. Ron was telling me how Jerry was always urging him to 'forget the feet' and campus things. Years later I definitely still subscribe to the 'forget the feet' philosophy!

Beyond his hard sends, Jerry's playful attitude really inspired me to have fun with my climbing. When I was 21, I had the rare opportunity to do a road trip with Jerry, Malcolm Smith and Marius Morstad. I remember being really impressed by Jerry's honed veteran experience, as he watched us for an hour trying a boulder in Rocky Mountain National Park before he then proceeded to flash it. I had a great time on that trip with those guys.

As I've got more experience, I know how important the psychological side of climbing is, and so Jerry's book can really help you to build your confidence, deal with pressure and improve your climbing.

So, thanks Jerry! *Mastermind* is a great book, and you should be really proud of how much you've influenced climbing, and in the way you did it.

Chris Sharma

Acknowledgements
Thanks to all the climbers who contributed to this book and everyone who racked their brains to make this book even better, most notably Professor Lew Hardy and Dr Noel Craine. Thanks to Hannes Huch, and Marion Hett, queen of graphic design, who made every page in this book into pure eye candy.

Chris and Jerry

© Jerry Moffatt

'HARD WORK BEATS TALENT WHEN TALENT DOESN'T WORK HARD.'

INTRO

As a child, I was competitive and wanted to do well and prove myself. At school, my achievements were not good – I am dyslexic and my reading and writing were bad. What's more, I also struggled with numbers. I was bottom of the class in all subjects even though I was trying my hardest. At the age of eleven, I couldn't read or write, and I had very low self-esteem and self-worth.

I passionately wanted to prove to myself and others that I was good at something. My school report at the age of seven said 'Jeremy is now pathetically anxious to succeed.' Thankfully, I was good at sports and I felt this was the area where I could do well and prove myself. This is where I got my real drive from. To some extent, it remains with me today.

I started climbing when I was fifteen and left school at seventeen with a few low-grade exam results. I went on a pursuit to become the best climber I could possibly be, fuelled by raw competitive drive and a desire to prove myself.

When I started climbing, it was all about strength, power and climbing all day, every day. As I matured, I grew to understand that there is more to climbing than the purely physical.

Despite the importance of strength, fitness, flexibility and movement, climbing is at its core a mind game. Sport is to do what your brain wants.

In climbing, there is no crowd to cheer you on. It's just you against the rock. It's a battle of holding it together when you're pumped out of your brain, slapping for the next move or the top.

I was mentally strong in my climbing until I did my first competition when the pressures and performance area were completely different to anything I had been used to. I underperformed and then I became fascinated with the process of mind and mental control, dealing with the pressure of performing at, and beyond, what you think are your limits. I realised that understanding how to make my mind work best under such intense pressure was the key to a winning performance. The difficulty was that information about sports psychology and the mental side of sports was hard to access before the days of the internet.

In *Mastermind*, I will share with you the different mental skills needed and used by climbers who have achieved great success over the past thirty years.

There are insights from a host of great climbers, the best in the world at this time, as well as my own thinking and research plus some academic insights from Professor Lew Hardy. Lew is Professor of Human Performance at Bangor University which has a worldwide reputation for research into elite performance. Lew is also an international mountain guide so totally understands climbing, and his work on sport psychology is world-renowned.

Bruce Lee has always been an inspiration to me. He said that there are three keys to success: persistence, persistence and persistence.

THREE KEYS TO SUCCESS: PERSISTENCE, PERSISTENCE AND PERSISTENCE.

BRUCE LEE

Progress is made in small steps and takes hard work. Putting in the right work on the mental side of your climbing will help you achieve your goals. The ideas outlined in this book will provide a framework to help you improve and hopefully get more fun out of your climbing.

My intention is that you will use this book like a guidebook. Get a pen out, underline what you like and think about what applies to you. You will need to experiment and see what works best. Use it actively and re-read it on a regular basis to make sure you keep working on the right things.

Ultimately, I hope that this book will help you get more success and enjoyment from your climbing, whether you are new to the sport or a professional.

JERRY MOFFATT + BORN 1963 + BEST CLIMBER OF THE 1980s + BE IT HARD ROUTES, TOUGH BOULDER PROBLEMS, ON-SIGHTS OR COMPETITIONS: NO ONE COULD BEAT HIS ALL-ROUND PERFORMANCE

Jerry on
*Le Spectre de
Surmutant*
(F8b+)

© Heinz Zak

EMPTY CUP

'MOVING,

BE LIKE WATER.

STILL,

BE LIKE A MIRROR.

RESPOND,

LIKE AN ECHO.'

BRUCE LEE

WISDOM

MIND CONTROL

Need for mind control:
When I talk about mind control, I mean the psychology of putting your mind and thoughts in the optimum place for a perfect performance.

A few times a year, things will occur that are really important and potentially challenging for you. It might be a job interview, speaking in front of a large audience or you're trying to redpoint a route you've been working on for a long time. Your head might be spinning with stress, maybe you didn't sleep well thinking about your project. This is when you need to know about mind control.

I would like to tell you my personal experience of why I sought to find out and desperately needed to know how my mind was working.

I never really had a problem climbing on the crags. I have always been strong mentally whether redpointing, bouldering or on-sighting. I loved the fact that if you fell off, for the most part, you could just try again. If I got frustrated, the anger would sometimes help to get me up a route. I knew I would always give one hundred per cent. There have been times when I have been climbing and people have been shouting up to encourage me. I used to think there is nothing you could say to make me pull any harder or give it more, absolutely nothing. I loved giving it everything I had. That's what climbing was to me.

In the late 1980s, competitions came along. I went to my first competition with an excellent track record on crags, feeling strong and confident. However, when I pulled on to the competition wall I found I had different thoughts in my head. Firstly, I didn't like climbing on plastic holds. This was an era before indoor walls became popular and I was inexperienced both climbing indoors and competing. Secondly, I didn't like being told exactly when I had to climb and I didn't like having an audience. I didn't want to fall off low down and I had a fear of failure. In short, so many things concerned me that I was unable to focus on my climbing.

I didn't perform as well as I wanted in my first competitions. I think I got a third place in a big competition and a first in a small one. Not all the best climbers were at the small one so to me it didn't really count. I incorrectly analysed where I thought my problems lay.

I trained harder, got stronger fingers, more power, got more consistent outside and lost weight.

In 1989, there was a big competition in Munich. I was living in Germany at the time and climbing well. I believed my performances on the rock should see me get a great result. I was already strong. The week before the competition I went on a low-carbohydrate/salt diet, getting my weight down to sixty-one kilograms (my natural weight now is seventy-five kilograms). The big day arrived and I climbed so badly on the first route. It was way beneath the grade I would normally on-sight easily. I was frustrated and angry with myself. Somehow, I got through to the semi-final, but only just. The next route was better for me, a delicate slab up to a big overhang. I had loved slab climbing on granite crags in America and also loved overhangs as it suited my bouldering strengths.

I qualified first on this. 'Thank heavens,' I thought to myself. I had now beaten all the other top competitors once, I just needed to do it again in the final. In the final, I walked out in front of the crowd not really knowing what or how I should be thinking; I had no point of focus. There was a delicate slab arête up to an overhang. I started up the slab. A couple of metres off the ground I was crimping hard on an edge looking up wondering what to do. The next thing my foot popped and I was hanging on the rope. I was absolutely devastated and went straight to the bar and drank beer as quick as I could. I took my performance really badly and barely slept for a week.

Looking back, I could not have handled the situation worse as I thought about my failure again and again. I was reinforcing the negative, telling myself things like 'I can't perform in competitions, I'll never win, I don't like performing in front of the crowd, what a waste of all that hard work and training, I am rubbish.'

Later, when I had calmed down, I reflected on my performance. It was obvious to me I should not compete again without trying to sort my mind out. I spoke to my parents, who said they had just read an article in the newspaper about a girl whose sport was archery. The girl had read a book on mental training and after reading the book went on to win consistently. We managed to contact her through the newspaper and obtain the book, *With Winning In Mind* by Lanny Bassham, an Olympic gold medallist in rifle shooting.

I had only one month to prepare for the next competition which was to be the first ever World Cup event. It was to be held in Leeds, England. Competitions in England at the time were not popular and had bad publicity. The older, more traditional climbers saw them as a threat to their sport because the early competitions had been set on normal crags. They thought that in the future the cliffs would be closed to hold competitions. Artificial climbing walls were very much in their infancy. It was my goal to win that Leeds competition. I wanted to prove competitions were a good thing and that British climbers could compete amongst the best in the world.

I knew that to climb better in competitions I needed a stronger mind for those situations.

'MIND CONTROL STARTS WITH A DECISION.'

JERRY MOFFATT

I threw myself head-long into Lanny Bassham's book, reading it daily, writing notes and doing as he suggested.

By the time the competition came along my head was in a different place. I didn't hope to win in Leeds; in my head I knew I was going to take the competition by the scruff of the neck and win, no matter what the cost. Simon Nadin, Didier Raboutou and I all touched the same holds high up in the final, so it ended up going to a super final.

Jerry winning the
first World Cup
event, in Leeds,
1989

© Ian Smith

I had everything rehearsed, visualised and was prepared for every eventuality. I knew I was going to win. It was my time, my competition. I then went out, completed the route and won.

I am absolutely sure that if I had not read Lanny's book I would not have won. I competed for about another year, consistently winning and ranking number one in the world in ASCI rankings.

When you consider it, in all sports nearly all the winning is done by a tiny percentage of the people competing. The same people win again and again. What's the reason for this? It's the way they think. They are confident, they have prepared well and they believe they will win. Mind control starts with a decision. For people who succeed that decision is: I'm going to be victorious and get it done. The exciting thing is that this mindset can help someone improve their performance and exceed their expectations whatever their realistic level of performance.

The same mindset that helps a 9a climber perform well can also help someone on their first 6b.

To become better at something you need education in the thing you are trying to get good at. I started my climbing career in the 1970s and since then I have met and talked to the very best climbers worldwide and some world champions in other sports. I have asked the questions and importantly listened to their insights to get that education to better myself.

In 1981, at the age of nineteen, I travelled to America which then had the hardest climbs in the world. I spent some of that winter climbing with John Bachar who was probably the best US climber at the time. I learnt a lot from him and started to lay down some of the foundations for my climbing career. I had never heard of stretching, warming up, rest days and eating well. I just figured the more I climbed, the better I would get, which had worked pretty well up to a point.

Throughout my career, I have done a lot of reading about training, diet and bodybuilding, which I found helpful for weight training. *Education of a Bodybuilder* by Arnold Schwarzenegger had just come out. Much later on in 1990, when I was back in the UK, I built a training board in my cellar in Sheffield. I framed some pictures of Schwarzenegger pumping weights, pushing through the pain barrier. Also in that picture was a quote from Arnie: 'I knew I was a winner. I knew I was destined for great things. People will say that kind of thinking is totally immodest. I agree. Modesty is not a word that applies to me in any way. I hope it never will.'

From a totally different angle, I enjoyed books on Zen, mind control and the writings of Bruce Lee who said: 'Become what you think. What you think largely determines what you will ultimately become.'

'WHAT YOU THINK LARGELY DETERMINES WHAT YOU WILL ULTIMATELY BECOME.'

BRUCE LEE

For me, this is a key thought.

I have interviewed a few world champions and some great climbers in the research for this book. Common thoughts run in the minds of these people. In basic terms, if you don't think you are going to do well, then it's quite probable that you are not going to do well. You might, but there is less chance of it. Be confident and just focus on climbing and having fun. If you can convince your mind that you are sure you can do it, then you have the best chance of succeeding.

SUCCESS

One definition of success could be winning. On the other hand a winning performance doesn't necessarily mean a win or top-out, or even completing a boulder problem.

For me success and a winning performance is achieving a standard you've not previously reached. Success rarely happens overnight, it is made with small steps.

You need to have a target. If you don't have a target or something to aim at, it's going to be hard to hit it.

In my experience, the most successful sportsman or woman turns out to be the one who works the hardest. People say, 'He was a natural,' then they say, 'He was always the first to start training and the last to finish.' It's hard to tell how natural someone is if they're just training way more than anyone else.

Here's how we learn the skills to succeed:

In the brain, we have two sets of neural networks that process reward and punishment. Reward would be a nice thing, punishment would be a bad thing.

All animals have these two sets of neural networks, not just humans.

That is how it is possible to train animals using reward and punishment. In normal conditions, for humans the reward/punishment networks are quite balanced. However, some people are extremely punishment-sensitive and not very reward-sensitive and vice versa. Somebody who is susceptible to reward and not punishment would respond very differently to somebody the other way round.

For example, if you're susceptible to reward then you would be highly optimistic, impulsive, confident and probably wouldn't see problems. Because you don't see problems you think to yourself, 'I can do this. Nothing can stop me.' You only see the reward of doing

'HE WHO KNOWS OTHERS IS WISE, HE WHO KNOWS HIMSELF IS ENLIGHTENED.'

LAO TZU

WISDOM

the thing and not the downside. You just want the reward as quick as possible.

If you are punishment-sensitive, all you would see is threats (a threat would be something that will inhibit your performance – a risk/hazard/danger). In such cases, you're not likely to be very confident; you see threats in every situation. You are likely to be cautious because all you see is a lot of things that could go wrong, not the reward.

In high-level performance, there is a lot of evidence that being punishment-sensitive is not a bad thing and potentially it's quite good.

Psychologists' best guess is that high-level performers have a burning desire caused by something earlier in their life which is locked away in the unconscious. They are extremely determined and committed people and do everything they can to succeed. They are just so determined that they will pick problems up early and deal with them. They can learn to identify and control these threats (distractions and things that can inhibit your performance) and put them in the right order, dealing with the most important ones first. This is a highly productive strategy.

In high-level performance, you have to see the threats or you are going to make terrible mistakes. The punishment-sensitive individual naturally picks up threatening images early and learns the skills to deal with them. The reward-sensitive individual needs to make a conscious effort to pick up the threats earlier. Once the threats have been identified, the skills needed to tackle and overcome them are the same.

The skills include confidence, concentration, visualisation, goal setting and planning. Learning them will undoubtedly enhance your ability, especially under pressure.

Keep an open mind. No one, however great, is beyond learning more. When striving for a goal, there is no point at which there is nothing left to learn. You need to be ready to learn, keep moving forward, refuse to lose, don't quit, take your time with quiet contemplation and find a way to succeed.

■ ∎ ■

ARISTOTLE

'KNOWING YOURSELF IS THE BEGINNING OF ALL WISDOM.'

'THE PRICE OF
SUCCESS.
HE WHO WANTS
TO SUCCEED
SHOULD LEARN
HOW TO FIGHT,
AND TO SUFFER.
YOU CAN REQUIRE
A LOT IN LIFE,
IF YOU ARE
PREPARED TO
GIVE UP
A LOT TO GET IT.'

BRUCE LEE

Adam Ondra
after sending
Pachamama
(F9a+)

© Hannes Huch

'For success, the mindset is most important. In my case I was super lucky to be talented, to have the support of my family, my parents driving me to the crag every weekend, and my training facilities were pretty good. I grew up in a positive environment. I was so positive about climbing it never felt like a sacrifice. I had my dream, to be a professional climber and be successful from when I was around seven or eight. I had so much fun on the way to getting there, even if I had failed to be what I wanted to be it wouldn't have been a waste of time. I wasn't sacrificing anything. I trained hard even when I was a little kid, but for me it was more fun going climbing. Training is like work, and climbing, that is a beautiful thing and something you love.'

ADAM ONDRA

WISDOM

WHAT DOES SUCCESS MEAN TO YOU?

LESSON

WHAT DOES SUCCESS MEAN TO YOU?

LESSON

MOTIVATION

Wolfgang Güllich
climbing in
Elbsandstein

© Gerhard
Heidorn

Motivation is what pushes or pulls an individual to start and direct sustained effort into an activity.

It's hard for me to talk about motivation without thinking of my friend Wolfgang Güllich who was one of the best redpoint climbers in the world; very sadly he is no longer with us. I can see him now sitting at the kitchen table drinking coffee, uttering the words 'at the moment I'm not motivated' in his thick German accent. His quote 'the mind is the most important muscle' is a great one.

'THE MIND IS THE MOST IMPORTANT MUSCLE.'

WOLFGANG
GÜLLICH

When Wolfgang was motivated, it was in the extreme. There was no stopping him. Then he would come back, usually from a success-ful trip and not climb for a few weeks, unmotivated. That's okay, up to a point. If you're not motivated, it's best to try and just do some-thing, just to keep things ticking over. Wolfgang was probably an ex-ception as he had so much natural raw power.

Chris Sharma has a kind of formula: 'Whatever time you take off, it takes the same to get back where you were.'

In other words, two weeks off and then you need two weeks to get back where you were. Rest is important though. It's important to think that you're actively doing something when you're doing noth-ing. Your body needs rest to regain energy. Don't feel guilty when you're sitting about doing nothing on a rest day. It's just as impor-tant as doing weights or getting pumped. It's a time to energise and re-motivate. You also want to avoid injury at all costs. There are not many things that can demotivate a climber more than an injury.

I never suffered from a lack of motivation when I was climbing. However, I varied my climbing a lot. I would do routes, on-sights and redpoints for a few months, then get into bouldering or training. I also travelled all the time. I had to mix it up. That variation and having a goal kept me motivated.

One of the best examples I know of motivation involves one of my oldest friends and climbing partner for many years, Ben Moon. Ben pretty much stopped climbing for about five years. His desire and motivation had gone. However, Ben felt he had more to give, missing the social side and health benefits. 'Just being in beautiful places' is how he sums it up.

There was a route he had always fancied doing that inspired him, *Rainshadow* (F9a). It was to be his motivation for getting back into climbing. In his late forties, he started to climb and train again.

After a year bouldering to build up core strength he started red-pointing again. He quickly did 8b which is remarkable in itself.

'I JUST THINK IT'S REALLY IMPORTANT TO HAVE A GOAL.'

BEN MOON

With hard work and unimaginable motivation, three years after climbing again at the age of forty-nine, Ben succeeded in redpointing *Rainshadow* at Malham Cove. In his words, 'I just think it's really important to have a goal.' You can read his account in the inspirational stories at the end of the book.

Setting a goal is the seed for motivation.

We will talk about this later.

Here are just a few other ways to keep motivated:

- TRAVELLING TO DIFFERENT AREAS
- GOING TO DIFFERENT GYMS AND INDOOR WALLS
- CHANGING CLIFFS
- DIFFERENT ROCK TYPES AND ANGLES
- CLIMBING AND TRAINING WITH MOTIVATED PEOPLE
- KEEP THINGS FUN

Ben Moon
working on
Northern Lights
(F9a)

© Steve Lewis

'I've never had a problem with motivation. Funny, what is important in climbing is variety. It's not only that I go climbing, I will do competitions or boulder. I really enjoy that I can pick right now what I want. Now I'm focused on redpointing, next could be bouldering or going to Yosemite. This is keeping it fresh, it's what keeps me motivated.

I think it's good for the overall performance. If I just went bouldering, I would probably go crazy. In bouldering, you learn something for sport climbing then you learn something from Yosemite and competitions and vice versa, so it's refreshing. In any climbing, you learn something new.

Motivation for me is climbing, its various sources let's say. In competitions, I make that my challenge. I'm competitive going for this competition. It means a separate challenge so I train hard. I shut myself in the gym for a couple of months and just train, train, train. Of course when I go into the competition, I want to show that I have trained hard. One part is to train hard enough and the

ADAM ONDRA

WISDOM

other part is to show that you can actually do it. It will never get boring. Sometimes I want to take a break from just being really focused, but I think that's the same with any sport. With sending routes like *La Dura Dura* I still have such good memories of just travelling there, just staying in the van. All these different ingredients made climbing so special for me. I even love the twenty-hour drive from the Czech Republic to Spain. For me, it's an integral part of climbing. That's what I learnt with my parents, it's what climbing is about. The most psyched I was, at the weekends, just sitting in the car thinking, "yes, I'm going climbing!"

Climbing all alone is definitely not so much fun. In training for instance, on endurance, I always have to train alone. To boulder, it's good that I can find some friends to boulder with. I would say for me it's best to climb sixty per cent with someone and forty per cent alone.'

'I think you have to be super passionate about what you want to accomplish. You have to have a clear motivation in that way. You have to truly love what you're doing and be inspired, that's the basis of it all. Once you are inspired then the motivation comes and once the motivation is there you do whatever it takes to achieve your goals.

It's the dream of any climber to look out of the window and see a great big limestone cave, but it's funny that does not necessarily make you climb hard. You can get lazy, and having a little bit of distance can make you want it and appreciate it.

I love climbing. I love finding new routes. I love the feeling of being at my highest level when your body is like a fine-tuned machine for climbing. Deeper than that, especially for someone like me, climbing is your identity. It's our vehicle for reaching our potential as human beings. Whatever we do is kind of irrelevant. I just want to lead a good life and realise my potential. That's how I have always felt and climbing is the way I can do that.

CHRIS SHARMA

The motivation is also all the routes we find. I think you constantly need new material to work with to be inspired. Going to the same cliff every day can be boring. You need ways to redefine yourself. It's not easy to stay psyched doing the same thing for twenty-five years, but in a way each time you go climbing you're different. You are coming to it from a new perspective in your life. That's the cool thing, the journey of life.'

WHAT WOULD MOTIVATE YOU MORE?

LESSON

BELIEF

Self-belief is like a core inner strength, like the foundations of a building. Imagine the foundations needed to build those large American skyscrapers.

With a great performance there is no question that the performer deep down has a very strong self-belief.

Confidence is different from belief. It can come and go and, like motivation, it can be fickle. Belief is knowing that no matter what, you are great.

A few years ago now, I remember seeing Chris Sharma compete in a bouldering competition in Salt Lake City. He was the favourite by a mile. He walked out to the last climb, the crowd cheered and then quietened in anticipation. Up to that point, no one had done the problem – a super-overhanging wall on slopers. Was it even possible? Chris had a good look at the problem, chalked up and pulled on. Then he promptly fell off! There was a shocked gasp from the crowd. His reaction? He turned round with a big smile and just started laughing. Many, including me, might have panicked, all sorts of negatives flowing into the mind. Not Chris. His belief in himself was just much stronger than that. He pulled on again and completed the problem and won. Seeing his reaction will always stick with me.

A climber free from excess tension while awaiting his performance is a typical sign of self-confidence and belief. It's a winning mind.

...He turned round with a big smile...

Chris Sharma

© Hannes Huch

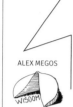

ALEX MEGOS

'When I'm in a negative state of mind I tend to climb worse. When I try to do it, I keep myself positive and that helps motivate as well. Staying positive and believing you can do it. The head is the most important thing, I feel.'

Confidence and, most of all, power of belief are things that run through the minds of people who succeed.

I go to quite a number of film festivals and always enjoy the mountaineering stories. One I witnessed this year really stands out. The belief shown by Sandy Allan (age fifty-seven) and Rick Allen (age fifty-nine), I think you will agree, was incredible. Their goal was to climb the Mazeno Ridge which includes seven summits above 7,000 metres, finishing up on the Diamir Face of Nanga Parbat. Also on the team were three Everest Sherpas, brought along not to carry, as Sherpas normally do, but as equal climbing members of Sandy's six-man-and-one-woman expedition team. They planned for eight days' food, which could possibly be stretched to ten. The ridge ended up taking fourteen days with the Diamir Face still to go. Discouraged and exhausted, Cathy O'Dowd and the three Sherpas descended. The food was down to half a packet of digestive biscuits. To make matters worse the flint on the lighter had worn out, which ruled out the use of the stove to melt snow for water. The consequences of dehydration increase the risk of frostbite, pulmonary and cerebral oedema. Sandy and Rick figured they could summit and return to base camp using fixed ropes in a day and a half. They went for it! It ended up taking three full days; the last part of the descent should have taken only three to four hours. Rick, in a state of exhaustion, had to sit down every few minutes, occasionally falling asleep. Sandy had to be strong for the team. Unbeknown to Rick, Sandy was hallucinating and starting to lose it. He could clearly see the White Rabbit from Alice in Wonderland hopping about in front of him. He didn't want to tell Rick so as not to panic him. They finally returned into camp at eleven o'clock at night.

They had conquered the last unclimbed ridge of the world's fourteen peaks over 8,000 metres. All previous attempts had failed. It's recognised as the most impressive British ascent on an 8,000-metre mountain in a generation. In England, every year we have awards for top sports personalities including best team. In my mind without question this was the most outstanding team effort of 2012. As it wasn't televised they didn't even get a mention. Sandy's book *In Some Lost Place* tells the epic story and it is a great read. I asked Sandy to comment on his belief that he could survive the final push to the summit.

This is what he said:

'Belief. That's an interesting powerful force in which I am no expert and never ever will be. From my own experiences, I think one has to have belief in oneself, the constantly spinning planets, the forces of nature and, from a mountaineer's perspective, the folks we climb with. That belief is innate for me since I was a kid running about the remote distilling Highland glens of Scotland and has developed with experience, which gives me strong confidence at high altitude, but does not necessarily apply to all walks of my life, such as in an office or around a committee table. One has to believe that you have earned your experience and you earn that experience through bad experiences. There lies the danger. How we experience trouble or avoid it – I call it "the climber's dilemma"!

SANDY ALLAN

As humans we have to acknowledge that smart people do stupid things; this applies to experienced smart people too, so it's important that we recognise this human factor in ourselves and find the discipline to manage it. We can perhaps be experts at a tiny proportion of our activities in our lifetime, but for the rest of the time we are really quite ignorant and so we use mental shortcuts to make our decisions.

SANDY ALLAN

We have to school ourselves to try and rule out assumptions. You have to take notice when your belief leads you to an assumption, check it out, look for facts and act on the facts, distinguishing emotions and zeal from actualities and not confuse them even under crippling circumstances such as high altitude.

In order to succeed, one has to be quite driven and determined. To stay alive, you have to recognise when your enthusiasm can make you reckless. You have to be positively sceptical, anticipate the dangers and have your own system to work to. No matter how bad the weather is or how cold my hands are I will always try to do things properly such as coiling the rope and racking my frozen gear in an organised manner trying to keep to a system. I know it may sound as though I am a bit of a nerd, but when the chips are down your body then acts automatically and does seem to follow the correct procedure (e.g. your body does the technical moves and you're not sure how, but it did it!).

Even though we are often tempted to take shortcuts, in a dangerous environment it's important we find the time to train our bodies to do things correctly in a procedure that we have self-developed through education, chats with others, taking into account their diverse opinions, including experience, until it's automatic. Belief is powerful, but it's terribly dangerous if we make our decisions based on experience only. For me, so far in my lifetime

I have eventually come to believe that not knowing is true knowledge, as that inspiring realisation
helps me find my way.'

DESIRE · COMMITMENT · WILL

We know that success takes perseverance. Something more powerful than motivation is the combination of desire, commitment and will. Will comes from the belief that 'I can do it'.

An example of commitment. A house is on fire, the top floor window is open and a child is inside. You run into the house to save a life, but the flames are too hot and you have to turn back. You cry for help, but get no answer. You try and find a ladder, but there isn't one. You go to the neighbour, but there's no one in. You go to the next house: 'Do you have a ladder?' 'No.' You continue on, etc.

You need desire and preparation to really succeed at something.

A true competitor is one who, when it's needed, gives all she or he has. That is commitment. Commit to everything: power, endurance, strength, flexibility, coordination, stretching, proper rest, hydration and diet.

Throughout the history of sport there are examples of people exerting extraordinary effort known as a 'clutch performance', and climbing is no different. In climbing terms after a big effort I would think to myself, 'I really pulled that one out the bag.' I found this often happened on the last try of the day. Normal effort would not have got me to the top. I used to think of it as if I were going into superdrive. No amount of pain in the fingers or forearms was too much. I had to keep going no matter what. When I was climbing like this it was like being in a highly emotional bubble moving in slow motion, almost euphoric with my mind focused completely in the present. With enough desire, it feels like you can keep going indefinitely to reach the summit.

The tale of Tommy Caldwell on *Dawn Wall* is truly an epic one, certainly the hardest free ascent of a big wall. It is a contender for the hardest route in the world. It's thirty-two pitches of mostly desperate climbing, over 760 metres, and it took almost twenty days of continuous climbing on the final push. More than that, he had to do it in winter to get the extra friction needed and he climbed in torchlight.

He spent seven years working on it, the hardest pitch being F9a.
I spent a few days with Tommy at a film festival.

Here is what he said about his desire and commitment on *Dawn Wall*:

'The funny thing is that I was not sure I truly ever believed I would climb *Dawn Wall*. I was purely focused on the journey and how it would mould me, and I was looking for an excuse to spend a lot of time in my favourite place in the world, Yosemite. Belief did play a role in the zoomed-in, move-by-move climbing. As in bouldering, you have to make yourself believe you are going to be able to do the moves before you actually do them. There is a funny paradox in big goals like *Dawn Wall*. You have to be inspired by the possibility, but let go of the outcome. Focusing on the growth and enjoying the journey allows that.'

TOMMY
CALDWELL

TOMMY CALDWELL + BORN 1978 + MOST FAMOUS FOR THE FIRST ASCENT OF *DAWN WALL* (F9A) ON EL CAPITAN, THE HARDEST MULTIPITCH IN THE WORLD, TOGETHER WITH KEVIN JORGESON HONOURED WITH THE *PIOLET D'OR* FOR THE FITZ TRAVERSE IN PATAGONIA

Leo Houlding, the mountaineer, climber and BASE jumper, is another person that stands out for me when I think about commitment. He is a real all-rounder and has mastered all forms of climbing from bouldering to extreme mountains with everything in between.

In 2004, Leo began BASE jumping and became a pioneer of para-alpinism which basically involves climbing up something big and jumping off the top. It has to be arguably the most dangerous sport in the world. We were having a meal a few years ago and he was telling me all about wingsuit flying. Then about BASE jumping Half Dome at sunrise, getting down in about five seconds doing 180 miles an hour. I asked him what it would be like skydiving out of a plane after doing something like that. He picked up his beer, had a sip and said 'About as exciting as that'.

I asked him his thoughts on commitment and how he gets his head together for an extreme jump.

Here's what he said:

'You could look at a BASE jump as the ultimate test of commitment. You're stood on top of a cliff and you're about to jump. Death is certain unless the equipment that you are entrusting with your life performs as expected and you are able to carry out the simple, but ultra-critical act of performing a stable exit, maintaining stability in free fall, deploying your canopy and piloting it to a safe landing.

In the 150 or so BASE "exits" that I have made, never once have I felt that my life was in peril. I have walked away from a great many where I thought my life was in danger, due to excess wind, poor visibility or some other unforeseen, unmanageable factor.

In all those jumps, never once have I so much as ever even broken a finger nail. I would like to put that margin of safety down to my proper preparation, training, judgement and skill. However, as more and more of my friends' lives have been ended prematurely by the deadly joy of BASE, I have begun to think that perhaps there is a larger element of luck involved than I may care to acknowledge and that sooner or later something bad is going to happen.

In air sports, they talk about "currency". It simply means how much you have been doing recently and it is extremely relevant to performance. You may have done 1,000+ BASE jumps, but none for the last three years and that may well put you in a more hazardous situation than somebody who has only ever done fifty, but they were all in the last three months. Every BASE jump is different every time. Obviously each site has its unique characteristics and each moment of each day its specific conditions. However, one's state of mind is equally, if not more, significant.

The first time you jump off a big cliff, it is extremely exhilarating to say the least. Copious amounts of adrenaline make an act as simple as holding your hand steady virtually impossible. Muscles are tense, breathing is quick and heart rate is through the roof. This is exactly the opposite of the state you should wish to find yourself in. When you have done fifty jumps in the last month and jumped the same site three times that day, that paralysing fear is completely gone, as has the surge of adrenaline.

Cool, calm and relaxed is how the experienced jumpers feel standing on the exit. They are focusing on flight performance and in no way fear for their lives.

LEO HOULDING

Often before you are about to jump somebody will say, "Nice and relaxed." Seems idiotically ironic, but it is totally true. However, I think perhaps herein lies the danger. Currency and experience effectively tame an initially wild beast of a sport. As the adrenaline of "student" exits and mellow flight lines subsides, the nature of the character of those attracted to what is seen by many to be the most dangerous of sports there is, encourages us to push further. Be it gnarlier exits, lower deployments or, particularly with wing suits, flying more and more aggressive proximity lines. We have all seen the incredible YouTube clips of pilots flying lines that look like they belong in a video game, slaloming trees and shooting

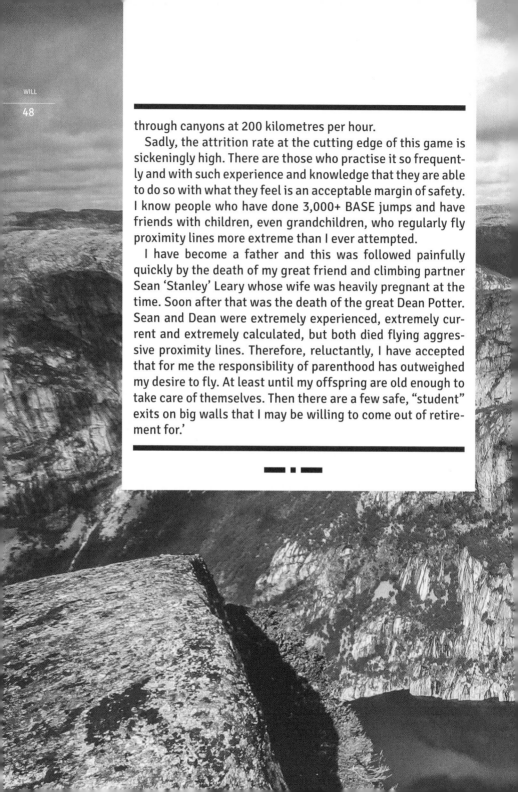

through canyons at 200 kilometres per hour.

Sadly, the attrition rate at the cutting edge of this game is sickeningly high. There are those who practise it so frequently and with such experience and knowledge that they are able to do so with what they feel is an acceptable margin of safety. I know people who have done 3,000+ BASE jumps and have friends with children, even grandchildren, who regularly fly proximity lines more extreme than I ever attempted.

I have become a father and this was followed painfully quickly by the death of my great friend and climbing partner Sean 'Stanley' Leary whose wife was heavily pregnant at the time. Soon after that was the death of the great Dean Potter. Sean and Dean were extremely experienced, extremely current and extremely calculated, but both died flying aggressive proximity lines. Therefore, reluctantly, I have accepted that for me the responsibility of parenthood has outweighed my desire to fly. At least until my offspring are old enough to take care of themselves. Then there are a few safe, "student" exits on big walls that I may be willing to come out of retirement for.'

Leo Houlding
performs an
'aerial' exit from
Kjerag, Norway.

© Chris 'Douggs'
McDougall

STRENGTH

Change weakness into strength.
If you want to move forward and improve your-self, sometimes it's best to step back and try to visualise yourself from someone else's viewpoint.

Cris, Ty, Amanda

Pick someone you respect and admire and then ask yourself, 'If they were watching me now, what would they say?' The point of this exercise is that you are self-coaching and analysing how you perform. You need to assess your performances, strengths and weaknesses so you know where you need to focus your attention.

In order to improve the level of your climbing, you need to pinpoint your weaknesses. Once you have found those weaknesses, then try to change them into strengths.

When I was nineteen, I spent my first winter in Joshua Tree National Park in California. At the time, it was pretty much the only place to go if you wanted to climb in the winter. I met John Bachar who was probably the best climber I had seen. His approach was very professional. He was super flexible, had great footwork and moved with real grace on the rock. It was impressive to see. I had finger strength and arm power, but lacked his precision in my footwork, smoothness and control. I had repeated all John's boulder problems in Joshua Tree; quite a few were second ascents, but still I wanted more.

My appearance was scruffy, my tent was a complete mess and I climbed like that. It was a total contrast to John. I decided it was time to change. The weaknesses in my climbing in my opinion were sloppy footwork and lack of attention to detail in my movement.

I cleaned out my tent and smartened up my appearance. If I wanted to be professional I had to look that way. I made a conscious effort to make my climbing more precise and controlled and eliminate my weaknesses. It definitely helped my climbing from then on.

Here's another example of when I had to have a word with myself. Surfing is a passion of mine since I retired from professional climbing. I was in the Canary Islands wanting to surf a rocky point break. On this particular day, the surf was massive. It was too big, out of control and nobody was out. Right on the inside, I noticed a small head-high wave which looked okay. I had only been surfing a few years up to that point and was a bit of a beginner – a kook in surfing terms. I jumped in and paddled across the bay lining up where I had seen the wave break with the massive waves a long way out behind me. I immediately felt myself drifting backwards in a rip. I was paddling pretty hard and slowly drifting backwards towards a horrific, huge shallow wave known as The Slab. I was getting nowhere, becoming distressed with my arms weakening. I could see my family sitting on the beach in the distance oblivious to the hell I was in.

I stopped for a second and thought to myself, 'What would a lifeguard say?' He would say, 'Don't panic, paddle to the side and get out of the rip.' It worked. I felt the release from the rip. Large white water waves were coming in. I paddled hard and belly-rode the first one I could to get in. I scrambled over the rocks exhausted. 'How was that, any good?' my wife enquired.

Be honest with yourself. Write down what you believe to be the weaknesses in your climbing. After you have done that, write down what your response will be to turn those weaknesses into strengths.

Some examples might be:

FINGER STRENGTH ON SMALL CRIMPS

> DO SOME STEEP CLIMBING ON LARGE FOOTHOLDS
> USING SMALL CRIMPS FOR FINGERS

CLIMBING IN FRONT OF THE AUDIENCE

> VISUALISE PEOPLE WATCHING YOU WHEN
> YOU CLIMB AND ENJOY IT

FOOTWORK ON SLABS

> TWICE A WEEK DO HANDS-FREE
> PROBLEMS ON SHEARS

MY PERFORMANCE IN THE EYES OF
SOMEONE ELSE

LESSON

- Remember how far you've come when you think abt how far there is to go

MY WEAKNESSES	MY RESPONSE

LESSON

MY WEAKNESSES	MY RESPONSE
Mental Game (Fear)	Do routes/ moves that scare me Positive self talk/belief Breathe!
Endurance	Do more top rope Climb slower Research!
Failing	Let go of outcome, focus on journey Laugh! Make it lighter Let go of your judgement/comparison to others

CONFIDENCE

Confidence is the belief in one's ability to achieve or do something.

The most common and obvious way to build confidence is through success – repeating something correctly which creates positive thought. Without doubt the most important determinant of confidence is how much you've succeeded in the past. However, there are also other ways to work on increasing confidence.

It's possible to get confidence from watching something as long as you can identify with the thing or person you're watching.

For instance, if I see Chris Sharma doing a route easily, it won't fill me with confidence that I can do it easily. If I watch somebody who I believe I am better than at climbing doing a route, that would give me confidence.

Another way to boost your confidence is using imagery. It will help your confidence when you visualise yourself doing something and succeeding in it.

When you visualise yourself doing something, you see the person do it and that person is you. It will enhance your belief that you can do it.

Talking positively to yourself and to others will enhance your confidence.

You don't necessarily have to use positive words in a rah rah corny way. For example, when out bouldering you might know how to do a move, but just can't do it. Perhaps you are starting to get frustrated; you might give your chalk bag a kick. Then you say to yourself: 'Stop being a complete idiot and do it!' For some people that could actually be quite positive. You're actually saying to yourself: 'You can do better than this and you can do it. Come on, do it!' That's a statement of confidence. It might also release some frustration because you're actually saying I know I'm better than this.

Since confidence is a belief, anything that says to you 'I believe I'm far better than this' announces your confidence. However, you could say the same words in a different manner with a pathetic tone in your voice and an air of defeat in it, which would do no good at all.

It's not the words, but the intention behind the words. In self-talk, it's always the intention to watch out for.

Emotion has an important role to play in climbing. The precise physiological patterns that accompany anger or that follow anxiety or happiness have not yet been established, but we do know they are all different.

The most obvious emotions to be concerned about with climbing are those of anxiety or fear.

Anxiety and fear are emotions that make us feel uncomfortable and tense. They are emotions we want to be relieved of as soon as possible. The key is how you interpret the anxiety and fear. With regards to emotional state and its effect on confidence, if you're frightened that may be good. You should be frightened if you are about to do something dangerous because that's what's going to keep you alive.

Embrace the fear, but control it. Don't try and suppress it. Face it head on and thereby you will be ready for it.

More experienced climbers will embrace the fear and ready themselves earlier than novices.

If you have a big competition coming up, you need to start worrying about it weeks in advance. Don't leave it to the day. Be anxious and imagine what it's going to be like to climb in front of all those people.

Prepare early, visualise and deal with it. As with the physical side of climbing, mental preparation is key.

The most important determinant of confidence is how much you have succeeded in the past. Importantly, failure reverses that.

The experiences of success and failure are not equal. In other words, when it comes to your confidence, the negative impact of one failure is not as equal in value as the positive impact of one success. There are big individual differences in this, but research has shown that for even the best sportspeople in the world, the ratio might still be as much as five successes being equal to one failure. There are lots of people at the other end of the spectrum who will need an even higher number of successes to equate to one failure. The popular norm is probably around thirty; it's huge. Failure smashes you quickly, while confidence is built up slowly from your successes. Knowing this very important piece of information, it's quite clear we need to reinforce success as much as possible. A great way to go about doing this is to imagine you have a bank account. For your accomplishments and successes you place them in your bank account. For every success you have, bank it, then reinforce it, tell yourself how well you've done and remember it.

It's incredibly important. You don't have to run around telling everybody how great you are, but internally you do need to tell yourself what a great job you've just done. No need for any modesty here like: 'I just did it because I was lucky', or 'It must've been the conditions.' Better self-talk would be: 'The conditions were bad, but I climbed just fantastic today – that's just like me. Good effort! I had no right to do that and I still did it.'

Further reinforcement I would advocate would be to write it down in a diary.

Just reinforce the hell out of every success you have. Never think of your failures, just don't go there.

Blame it on the conditions, your skin, or whatever you can think of and forget it. Build up that bank account and keep making those deposits to build your successes which in turn will improve confidence.

When you've got thirty successes in there it might just be enough to give you the confidence you need for a big on-sight. Remember, twenty-eight might not be quite enough. You need them all.

Somebody who really struck me as being exceptional in this matter is Adam Ondra. He just banks every success. Right from the word go on his warm-up he will be thinking things like: 'I feel good today. That felt easier than normal.' He uses so much positive self-talk. Not only that, he also expels negative thoughts. If he didn't feel good on the warm-up, his thought process would be: 'The conditions aren't great. I felt good yesterday and I can't have lost it since then.' He will then think about how great he felt yesterday.

Sometimes he will even go back a couple of weeks and pick out a great day and just think about that right before he starts climbing. His success bank account is absolutely bursting!

If by reading this book I can just help you build your confidence and nothing else, this will have a very positive impact on your climbing. Confidence is such an important factor in all sport.

■■ ■ ■■

So to summarise, these are the ways to boost confidence:

- YOUR SUCCESSES AND BANKING THEM
- VISUALISE EXPERIENCES OF SUCCESS
- TALKING POSITIVELY TO OTHERS AND YOURSELF

Alex Megos on
Action Directe
(F9a)

© Claudia
Ziegler

**WRITE DOWN YOUR SUCCESSES,
BANK THEM!**

LESSON

CONCENTRATION

Concentration is a narrowing of the mind and focusing on one specific thing, a form of exclusion.

It's much easier to concentrate if you're confident. For example, if you have no confidence then you will get distracted by negative thoughts and therefore your concentration will be poor. Alternatively, if you have very high confidence you can become complacent and lack focus, and concentration can also be negatively affected.

Confidence and concentration are related, but not in a straightforward way. It's not as simple as the more confident you are the more you'll concentrate. That works only up to a certain point.

Concentration is about selectively attending to what's important for you to perform a certain task. There are two parts to concentration and they're dealt with in different parts of your brain.

One part of your brain is used to select information you are going to attend to. The other part of the brain is used to inhibit the things you do not want to attend to. When you are climbing at your limit you will be very focused on the piece of rock in front of you. That is the thing you want to attend to; your field of focus is very narrow. There are huge amounts of things that you inhibit, the things you don't want to attend to. For instance, you will inhibit the memory of the moves you have climbed already, the moves still to come, what you are going to have for dinner. You want to inhibit everything that's not involved with you making the next move.

If your attention gets drawn to falling, where you are going to land, what you are having for dinner, then you are not concentrating. When you are concentrating your mind is not open, it's really a small focused area.

Concentration requires you to inhibit what you don't want and selectively attend to what you do want.

We selectively attend to the things we think are most important to us, but these may not always be the most important things. For instance, a novice would probably focus on where they are going to land and what will happen if they fall. That's one of the reasons why they struggle. Other reasons would obviously be strength, technique and inexperience. Experienced climbers will inhibit those things, as they are more confident and know they will land correctly. They are more likely to focus on the detail of how they are going to place their fingers precisely on the next hold, working out body shape and getting the dynamics of the move done correctly.

In climbing, the time when you need super-intense concentration is when you are soloing. There is no room for error. Pinpointing the challenge is clear. Do not fall. I like John Bacher's quote 'Soloing is a serious business, because you can be seriously dead.'

I used to do a lot of solos. In the early 1980s, I also wanted to climb the most dangerous trad routes I could. For months on end, every day I climbed without ropes. I wanted to put myself in a situation and be comfortable with the fact that any mistake could be fatal.

'ONE OF THE GREATEST CAUSES OF FAILURE IS LACK OF CONCENTRATION.'

BRUCE LEE

Sometimes when climbing I'd just be so focused and not really aware of the situation. Then at the top, looking over the edge, I'd think, 'Ooh, that looks scary', while not being even the slightest bit scared while climbing. Such was the level of my concentration.

I would say this: soloing is very dangerous and I am not advocating people go soloing armed only with a chalk bag, shoes and one hundred per cent concentration. You have to weigh up the risks, train and prepare thoroughly for this type of climbing. Accidents can happen when the hard climbing is done and you are just soloing an easy route down or descending a gully. The adrenaline has gone, along with the concentration, and that is when mistakes can be made.

Remember this from Bruce Lee: 'One of the greatest causes of failure is lack of concentration.'

Shooting clays with a shotgun takes great skill. In theory it's simple: shoot and break one clay, remember how you did it and repeat it. The best in the world need to shoot pretty much perfect scores to win. You can imagine as the pressure builds you need flawless technique and it's imperative to keep up your concentration. I have had a shotgun since I was fourteen years old and love the mental challenge of shooting clays. I have lessons with double world champion David Beardsmore. In practice, Dave has shot over 1,000 clays without missing a single one, and 952 straight in competition.

Dave's thoughts on keeping up concentration:

'The world championship went to a shoot-off, with me against one other guy. We both shot 200 straight [no misses] the first day. We returned the next morning to fight it out again; my opponent and I shot the first eighteen with no mistakes. Then he missed the nineteenth target, a very difficult fast and low, right-to-left which had to be shot very aggressively without hesitation. It was my chance; if I could break the next eight targets I would be world champion. My mental game is all about my pre-shot routine. I put my focus into that, doing exactly the same thing each time before I shoot. I can then concentrate on breaking the next target presented in front of me. There is nowhere for any negativity to enter my head. I smashed the next eight and won.'

Margo Hayes
concentrating

© Hannes Huch

'For me, the hardest part is to get into the zone or flow, when I don't think in words or sentences. When all my movements are on autopilot, moves are driven by intuition or experience. In my perspective, the mind is only there to make it worse. If your mind is one hundred per cent then your performance can be close to your potential one hundred per cent. If your mind is bad and you are nervous and there are some doubts then maybe you're climbing at fifty per cent. I would describe it as: if I enter the zone the mind is not there, my mind is on holiday. Intuition is not necessarily better than my mind, but it's most probably better.'

ADAM ONDRA

Adam Ondra

© Claudia
Ziegler

UNCONSCIOUS THOUGHT

Neuroscientists estimate ninety-eight per cent of the brain is occupied with the unconscious. This unconscious part of the brain does things like keep your heart going, work your digestive system, activate your muscles and much more.

The top end of brain activity enables you to have thoughts that you are aware of; that is conscious thought. This conscious thought enables you to hold temporary information to do tasks. When the working memory has performed that task it can move on to another one and the working memory slate is wiped clean.

When you first start climbing you will be most likely doing that consciously. You'll probably think: 'I need to get up that, put my hand here, my foot there etc.' Your conscious mind will conjure up the sequential order of movements you need to make. Working memory holds the sequence in your consciousness, enabling you to set off and begin climbing.

As was famously argued by Freud, it seems apparent that the unconscious mind can have a big influence on behaviour. There has been some important research leading sport psychologists to believe unconscious processes underpin all elite performance. If you are just a happy person who is completely satisfied with life, why on earth would you do all that hard training and work and commit to be a super-elite athlete? What will be the point most people would just think, 'I am pretty happy, I'll hang out with my friends, go for a coffee or go down the pub.'

There has to be a driver for super-elite performance and that drive is almost certainly unconscious.

The thought process that says 'I can't finish without winning' will be common amongst elite sport people. Popular thought is that very high-level performance is driven by positive things. Actually it's probably not, it's more likely to be something negative hidden in the unconscious that drives the fear of failing. 'I can't finish not winning. I'm losing and need to avoid losing. I will conquer this. I will not be beaten!' That's where the drive comes from. Fear is a great motivator, if it's controlled. All your thoughts are generally regarded as conscious.

The unconscious mind is where you generate and store information needed for your skill.

An example of an unconscious skill is when someone throws a ball for you to catch. First, your conscious mind thinks, 'catch it'. Then unconsciously you watch the ball, your hand reaches out and your fingers tighten as the ball hits your palm. The unconscious mind is where skills are stored, like riding a bike, driving a car, swimming, running, walking and so on. Your unconscious mind does not reason independently, it just does what the conscious mind thinks.

However, very importantly the unconscious follows the thoughts and desires of the conscious mind. That is why it is critical to control what your conscious mind is thinking before any type of sport activity.

The more you climb the more unconscious skills you will be acquiring. It's like building an encyclopaedia of climbing in your mind. The reason an experienced climber will work out a move quickly is because he or she has either seen a move like that or done one like that before. For this reason, bouldering is a great way to start and develop your climbing because you can just do so many different types of moves in a session. This quickly builds up to a repertoire of moves. Of course, in climbing other strengths will help greatly, like finger power, core strength, arm strength, flexibility, footwork, balance and so on. These are your skills, and your skill value is the grade you potentially can climb. It is for you to go out there and work on in your training and climbing.

If you can keep your mind completely focused on succeeding at the task you want to complete, it is not possible at the same time to picture failing at that task. You need to get all that fear of falling, failing and uncertainty assessed and then inhibited prior to starting the task. When I say inhibited I mean obstructed, repressed or prevented from entering your conscious mind. Put all your focus into the move presented in front of you. So in principle it is easy.

Repel and inhibit negative thoughts and picture positive thoughts to control your inner environment.

That is why tools like visualisation, staying in the present and routines before you climb are so important. It is critical what your mind pictures and thinks.

■— ■ —■

CONSCIOUS THOUGHT

Conscious thought is accessible to you right now. It's what you can talk about, it's in your head and it's accessible.

Conscious thought can only focus on a limited amount of things at one time – like this chapter, which is incredibly important.

Very good evidence from scientific research has shown most people can focus on seven things plus or minus two, so somewhere between five and nine.

That's stuff you can hold in conscious memory while doing something else. It's almost certainly true that the smaller amount we hold in the consciousness the better we can focus on one thing. For instance, if you started trying a very difficult dynamic move, if you only thought of one part of the move you probably would not make the move, as you wouldn't do all the other stuff like getting your body in the correct position. You're more likely to be making sure your feet stick on take-off, how you throw your hips in, get the distance and hit the hold you're jumping for in a precise manner.

The more you can synthesise things down to one thing and picture it in a single concept the better, because you will be able to focus and concentrate clearer on the thing you're trying to attain.

This single concept is called a 'process goal': to capture just one thing in a single vision. Getting a process goal is so important and will really help your climbing. So with regards to the dyno, if you concentrate on sticking the hold you're going for and assume if you do that everything else will take care of itself that is a 'process goal'. That's the best way to maximise yourself doing things because you've simplified it down to one thing; obviously it can't be less than one. You leave other parts of your body to deal with all the other things. You will know yourself as you work a move repeatedly that certain things gradually take care of themselves. You work it all out in your mind just how to make the move. I think that's natural, but you are not always aware of it. The smaller the number of process goals we have in our minds the better.

One example I can think of for an intense process goal is when I did *Dominator* in Yosemite. It's a three-move boulder problem, the first being the hardest. I recall it took me about three days to do the last two moves, although I didn't manage to link them. I could not do the first move, but was getting close. It involved getting a pinch-grip with my right hand and jumping up and left to a very small openhanded three-finger edge; it's very steep with nothing really for your feet. As I got the hold with my left hand I just couldn't hold the swing. I worked my right hand on the pinch, making sure I had it perfect. I thought about my feet: were they in the best position? As I made the jump, I tried to hold the swing to get the body tension. I was struggling to make the distance and get the finger hold precisely as I wanted it.

I was obsessed with it and racked my brain over how I could do the move. I had a rest day and went for a massive walk to the top of the Lost Arrow Spire, eating only a tiny salad that evening so I could be super light. I can remember being so hungry, but just didn't want to eat. It was May and it was really hard to get good conditions. I didn't want to return in September when the conditions would be better. I even put my chalk in the microwave in the hope I would get extra purchase (forget it, it doesn't work!).

As I tried the problem next day it was obvious to me that I had to focus completely on getting the finger edge for my left hand absolutely perfectly. That was my process goal. I just couldn't get it as I needed. I contemplated what I was going to do: 'If that edge was a pocket I think I could get it.' So I got my finger tape out; put a strip to the right and left of the hold so it looked like a pocket. My focus and process goal was only to get that hold perfect. I wasn't thinking about anything else even doing the problem. I chalked up, focusing on the pocket I'd made – 'calm, focused aggression'. There were probably eight or so people sitting behind watching. It didn't bother me at all as long as they were quiet and didn't shout while I was climbing. You could hear a pin drop. My entire world focused on getting that finger hold precisely. I made the move first go, went straight into the second and third, and in a split second I'd done *Dominator*. What a rush! I believe it was the first Font 8b.

With regards to coaching, this process goal aspect is often overlooked or not properly understood.

It's very rare a coach would give a pupil just one thing to think about. The performer's job is to do the task they're attempting, solely to do it to the best of his or her ability. The coach's job is to find one thing that will help them to do that task the best they can. They don't need to know how great you are, everything you know about the task they are trying to do or all your amazing knowledge of sport psychology. It simply won't help. Just giving them one process goal to focus on is really going to help.

There is a phenomenon called conscious processing which is when we learn to do something new for the first time. Take bouldering for instance: in the early stages of learning we will make uncoordinated jerky movements. We have to consciously control movements, breaking things down into little chunks of movement and consciously controlling each one. As we become more skilled we learn to do these things automatically in an unconscious way, enabling us to join the movement together effortlessly. It then doesn't entail using conscious processing (breaking each move down consciously), as it's done unconsciously so requires less effort. When you've done lots of climbing you make all sorts of moves flow easily together unconsciously using muscle memory because you are used to doing so. Especially when under pressure and possibly when you try too hard, there may be a tendency to revert back to those rules we used consciously to learn the thing we are trying to do. The logic being, that's how we learnt to do it so it must be correct. We re-employ those explicit rules, consciously breaking the moves down into chunks and thereby perform like a novice.

Examples in climbing would be using excessive forces: movements become less fluid and you might generally have a lack of accuracy when placing fingers and feet on holds. On routes, redpoint or onsight, this is very important because if you are using excess energy early on you get pumped at the top and fall.

It's important to trust the skills you have learnt and let the unconscious simply do the work. Your job is to narrow your focus on the next move you have to solve. Conscious processing is just another thing to be aware of.

Jerry on
Dominator
(Font 8b)

© Kurt Albert
(RIP)

SELF-IMAGE

Self-image is the way you perceive yourself. The way you think you are and what you feel comfortable in doing.

This is one of the main ingredients that we need to get working correctly for optimum performance.

These thoughts you have are all part of your history, your upbringing, the way you were taught, influences from friends and parents, good and bad things that have happened in your life.

The reason it's a vital part is because if you think it's not like you to do a grade of route or flash a certain type of problem, it's going to make it very hard to do it.

Your self-image will have an expected performance zone in which you normally perform.

For instance, if you're inexperienced and playing pool and you start knocking all the balls in at some point your mind will think 'What's happening? I never do this, it's not like me'. It feels uncomfortable. Then you will start missing and your mind will think, 'That's more like me'; your performance will feel more like you imagine you ought to play. Let's call that your expected performance zone.

You need to believe that your expected performance zone is as high as your skill value, if not higher.

In other words, performing to your full potential every time and in all pressure situations. In sport, your actions will follow your mental thoughts and images.

In climbing, you may hear people talking themselves down, which indicates a problem with self-image. 'I can't climb in the morning. I can't climb on polished rock. I climb well in qualifications, but always blow the final.' Thoughts like this put you at a huge disadvantage.

This was my problem when I started doing competitions. I would tell people, thereby telling myself, 'I don't like competitions. It's not like climbing on real rock. I climb much better outside.' Then I attempted to win in Leeds in 1989. I had been working really hard on my self-image. I convinced myself that I loved competitions and did my best climbing in them. I had also persuaded myself that I loved climbing on plastic, climbing indoors, waiting hours in the isolation zone. I had changed my self-image and my expected performance zone. I did that by creating a positive declaration which I talk about in the next chapter.

Later that year, I remember speaking to François Legrand at a competition. He was an amazing climber with immense talent, but he had failed to win or beat me. He told me just before a final, 'I climb so well up to the semi-final, then always blow the final.' He said his ambition was to beat me once that year. His self-image and expected performance zone expected him to fall off in the final. When he said this, I knew I had the better of him because his self-image was holding him back. I also knew as soon as he had won a final that I would be in big trouble!

François climbed fantastic, beating me at the end of the year in Arco in Italy. He then had belief as his self-image changed to 'I climb great in the final.' François then went on to win five world championships to become the best lead competition climber to date. The first win is always the hardest. You are so happy after, you think about it all the time; picturing all those great memories just rein-

'THE CONSCIOUSNESS OF SELF IS THE GREATEST HINDRANCE TO THE PROPER EXECUTION OF ALL PHYSICAL ACTION.'

BRUCE LEE

forces success so brilliantly. I think that's the reason it is easier to win the second time.

You need to identify how you can improve your self-image.

Take the time and write down where you think you might have a problem. Then write down how you want to be. If you are not happy with a particular self-image then you must replace it with one that is in direct opposition to the self-image you want to change. For instance, if you think you don't perform under pressure your new self-image is 'I love pressure. That is when I perform at my best.' I cannot stress how important it is you get things written down. If you have a problem, things become clearer; it will help you to see things in black and white.

When I was travelling, climbing and competing I was continually writing down lists and ideas. When I started writing this book I had a look through my diary from 1990. In the back, to my surprise, were some papers with my thoughts at the time.

Here is what I wrote on self-image:

I PERFORM BETTER IN COMP THAN CRAG. 4 TASKS:
- WILLING TO UNDERGO CHANGE
- IDENTIFY HABITS AND ATTITUDES THAT
  NEED TO BE CHANGED
- SET NEW SELF-IMAGE WHICH IS IN
  DIRECT CONFLICT WITH THE OLD SELF
- EXCHANGE NEW FOR OLD SELF-IMAGE

then I went on to say:

'Control writing and talking, never talk failure, remember good. Take something you're poor at and make it your best attribute.'

Once you have identified the changes you need to make in your self-image I can show you how it is possible to replace them with a positive declaration. It is not easy, as it can feel emotionally uncomfortable. You have to be willing to undergo the change and only you can do that. If your self-image does not like climbing in front of a big audience and you want to change, it is going to require work and input from you and it's not going to happen overnight.

— ▪ —

HOW I AM

LESSON

HOW I WILL BE

HOW I AM

LESSON

HOW I WILL BE

POSITIVE DECLARATION

A positive declaration is a positive conscious thought with the motivation to change a belief.

One of the hardest things to change is your self-image and to improve your expected performance zone. You should be ready for a great performance, your mind should be thinking, 'This is normal for me. This is how I expect to perform.'

This is one of the most powerful statements I know:

'The more we think about, talk about, and write about something happening, we improve the probability of that thing happening.' (Lanny Bassham, *With Winning In Mind*.)

I have found this to be absolutely true. Personally, writing things down has been extremely important. If you're doing revision for an important exam you wouldn't just read the stuff you need to learn, you would write down the important things, probably more than once. You are then likely to look at it and think, 'This is what I need to remember.' It's a similar thing you need to do if you want to improve your self-image and expected performance zone.

You need to identify how you would like to perform, but it must be realistic and in keeping with your skills.

Write down a short list of things you would like to achieve on the rock, and pick out the most important ones and the areas that need work. These need to be linked together into a couple of paragraphs summing the whole thing up, and put your long-term goal at the bottom. What you have written is a positive declaration.

It is up to you then how much you want that declaration to become true. If you write it down, read it once and never look at it again obviously it's not going to do much good. If, however, you think about it a lot, read what you've written down every day and talk about it, it's much more likely to happen. Remember, the more we think about, talk about and write about something happening, we improve the probability of that thing happening.

'THE MORE WE THINK ABOUT, TALK ABOUT AND WRITE ABOUT SOMETHING HAPPENING, WE IMPROVE THE PROBABILITY OF THAT THING HAPPENING.'

LANNY BASSHAM

Doing a positive declaration is the best way to change the way you think.

These thoughts may be quite personal and possibly not the kind of thing you want to share with other people. That's fine, you don't have to shout it from the rooftops.

I wrote one in 1989 and 1990 and shared it with no one except my girlfriend at that time. I did not want to put extra pressure on myself by making statements about how I was going to win or do a particular grade of route. If I was asked how I was climbing I might answer, 'Doing okay, not that fit', but importantly, as I said it I would be thinking, 'That's rubbish, I'm in the best shape of my life.'

Here is one of my positive declarations which I found on a piece of scrap paper in the back of my 1989 diary. I don't remember writing this particular one, but it must have been just before Leeds because underneath there was lots of writing about how I was going to win that competition.

■ ∎ ■

Jerry's positive declaration:

I AM THE BEST COMPETITION CLIMBER IN THE WORLD

I ALWAYS SUCCEED

I ALWAYS FLASH 8A (HARDEST GRADE AT THAT TIME
TO BE ON-SIGHTED)

MY FOOTWORK IS PRECISE AND EFFICIENT

I MOVE ON THE ROCK FAST AND GRACEFULLY

I HAVE PLENTY OF TIME TO WORK OUT MOVES BECAUSE
MY RECOVERY IS SO GOOD

I CAN DE-PUMP EVERYWHERE

I AM THE STRONGEST AND FITTEST CLIMBER IN THE WORLD

I WILL WIN LEEDS 1989!

When you have written one down and you're happy with it, copy it down on four or five cards. Put these around the house where you are likely to see them at regular times of the day. Next to the fridge, the kettle and your bed are good places. When you read them, visualise what you have written and believe it.

JERRY MOFFATT

WISDOM

Doing a positive declaration is pretty intense and I can appreciate it's not for everyone, but believe me they can be life-changing.

'KEEP IT POSITIVE, POSITIVE, POSITIVE!'

MY POSITIVE DECLARATION

MY POSITIVE DECLARATION

MY POSITIVE DECLARATION

MY POSITIVE DECLARATION

MY POSITIVE DECLARATION

MY POSITIVE DECLARATION

MY POSITIVE DECLARATION

MY POSITIVE DECLARATION

MY POSITIVE DECLARATION

MY POSITIVE DECLARATION

MY POSITIVE DECLARATION

MY POSITIVE DECLARATION

MY POSITIVE DECLARATION

MY POSITIVE DECLARATION

MY POSITIVE DECLARATION

MY POSITIVE DECLARATION

MY POSITIVE DECLARATION

MY POSITIVE DECLARATION

MY POSITIVE DECLARATION

MY POSITIVE DECLARATION

MY POSITIVE DECLARATION

MY POSITIVE DECLARATION

MY POSITIVE DECLARATION

MY POSITIVE DECLARATION

Margo Hayes on
La Rambla (F9a+)

© Greg Mionske

GOAL SETTING

It is no secret that it is essential to have a goal. I would say most ambitious people have some sort of goal.

Sometimes goals can be mistaken for wishful thinking, and for this reason your goal should be absolutely realistic. There is no point when you start climbing thinking you want to be the best in the world. Right at the start that's pretty unrealistic, even though it's a great thought. Only when you are the best in your country can you start thinking about it.

Your goal should represent what you wish to happen in the future and it should have some idea of a timescale or deadline.

I feel it would be beneficial to write it down. After you have identified your long-term goal, you need to create some short-term goals or targets which need to be achieved, which will enable you to reach your final goal. If you don't set deadlines and have timescales for these goals, then what you are doing is just creating a vague outline of what you want to do.

With experience, it's maybe not quite as critical to get things written down, as the vision you have will be clearer in your head. I would still advocate putting something down in writing to make sure you don't cheat on yourself and change deadlines or short-term goals.

What I would say is that your goal absolutely has to be realistic. If you set unrealistic goals, it could put too much pressure on you and could take away the pleasure from your climbing.

Your dream and goal should be the process of doing the route and succeeding, rather than just to be able to look back and say you've done it.

It's really important that your climbing experience is an enjoyable one.

The more fun it is the easier it will be to put in the hours of training, driving around and climbing that are required to improve. However, don't stress yourself out too much.

As Marc Le Menestrel says, 'Don't be prisoner of your goals, they are all just a mental construction to reveal what really matters: the journey itself. Goals should be at the service of climbing, not the contrary.'

What you're looking for in setting a goal is progression and reinforcement.

When writing your goal and short-term targets you should describe what you want to achieve and never what you want to avoid. Do not write something like 'stop climbing when I feel weak'. Keep it positive, positive, positive. Never give up on a goal, even if it doesn't go well at first. Unforeseen things might happen, like injury or work commitments. Progression is never made on a sliding scale going straight upwards. You're always going to have some days that are not as good as you would expect. That's fine, it happens to everybody. Try and make at least one definite move forward each day, even if it's just a small move like visualisation. That's a positive move in the right direction. I would not set goals too far in the distance. For me, one year in advance is enough. After you have reached that goal, it's time to set another. When writing your goal, write it as if you have already achieved it. For example, if you want to climb F8a you would write down 'GOAL: I am an 8a climber by October.'

If you are a 7c climber and you want to climb 8a, here is how you might write down your goal. Climbing 8a is a realistic goal in a twelve-month period if you have not been climbing too long and you are redpointing 7c. Your short-term goals might be as follows:

Months 1–3 – redpoint fifteen 7c routes

Months 4–6 – start work on and redpoint a 7c+

Months 7–8 – do five more at 7c+

Months 9–12 – identify 8a project and get it done.

Hopefully, you can see how goal setting works and how much clearer it is when it is written down. You should be able to see how to go about achieving your goal. Next you need some sort of a plan of how you are best going to achieve hitting those intermediate goals or targets.

■ ∎ ■

'DON'T BE A PRISONER OF YOUR GOALS, THEY ARE ALL JUST MENTAL CONSTRUCTIONS TO REVEAL WHAT REALLY MATTERS: THE JOURNEY ITSELF. GOALS SHOULD BE AT THE SERVICE OF CLIMBING, NOT THE CONTRARY.'

MARC LE MENESTREL

WISDOM

'I just set goals such as "I want to win the World Cup" or "I want to climb 9b+ or 9c". It's usually a few simple goals. I usually achieve the goals I set for myself. I hope it doesn't sound like boasting. I'm ambitious and if the path to the goal gets too difficult I am easily frustrated.

With a training plan it's different. I would set a basic training programme for a competition together with Patxi [Patxi Usobiaga is Adam's coach] who I'm working with specifically for a goal. We would have a rough plan to begin with and be very precise for the last few weeks. I pressurise myself a lot and I think I'm good at handling that. I put a lot of effort into it.

ADAM ONDRA

If you are a hobby climber (you have a hard job and you just want to climb and have fun in your free time) in that case it could be dangerous to set a very high objective in a goal. It's supposed to be fun in your free time and it could be just too frustrating if you set your goal too high.'

'When it's time to get stuff done I'll focus and make it happen. For me, a big goal was to climb 9b+. It was a big goal of mine to climb *La Dura Dura* because I just had to push myself. I don't think it was necessarily the grade for me. I've been pretty talented as a climber and been able to do hard things without having to work so hard, but that route was kind of an example to myself. To push through that comfort zone and see if I could do something a step beyond.'

CHRIS SHARMA

MY GOAL FOR THIS YEAR: I'M AN F8A CLIMBER 1ST OCTOBER

LESSON

REDPOINTING 1S 7C ROUTES →

REDPOINT 7C+ →

	WK 1	WK 2	WK 3	WK 4
JANUARY				
FEBRUARY				
MARCH				
APRIL				
MAY				
JUNE				

> **'TO STRIVE ACTIVELY TO ACHIEVE SOME GOAL GIVES YOUR LIFE MEANING AND SUBSTANCE.'**

BRUCE LEE

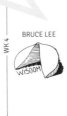

WISDOM

JULY   WK 1   WK 2   WK 3   WK 4

AUGUST   WK 1   MORE 7C+   WK 2   WK 3

SEPTEMBER   WK 1   FIND MY BA PROJECT   WK 2   WK 3

OCTOBER   WK 1   CLIMB MY BA PROJECT   WK 2   WK 3

NOVEMBER   WK 1   WK 2   WK 3

DECEMBER   WK 1   WK 2   WK 3   WK 4

MY GOAL FOR THIS YEAR:

LESSON

JANUARY — WK 1 — WK 2 — WK 3 — WK 4

FEBRUARY — WK 1 — WK 2 — WK 3 — WK 4

MARCH — WK 1 — WK 2 — WK 3 — WK 4

APRIL — WK 1 — WK 2 — WK 3 — WK 4

MAY — WK 1 — WK 2 — WK 3 — WK 4

JUNE — WK 1 — WK 2 — WK 3 — WK 4

JULY   WK 1 ——— WK 2 ——— WK 3 ——— WK 4

AUGUST   WK 1 ——— WK 2 ——— WK 3 ——— WK 4

SEPTEMBER   WK 1 ——— WK 2 ——— WK 3 ——— WK 4

OCTOBER   WK 1 ——— WK 2 ——— WK 3 ——— WK 4

NOVEMBER   WK 1 ——— WK 2 ——— WK 3 ——— WK 4

DECEMBER   WK 1 ——— WK 2 ——— WK 3 ——— WK 4

PLAN

Now you have a goal with a date, you have something to aim at. You can now detail a plan of the best way of hitting the bullseye for that target and achieving your goal.

Before we start, it's very important that for the most part you enjoy the whole process of the plan. If you stop enjoying it or if it gets too stressful you can always adjust your plans. When you are creating your plan, you need to think about all the things you could do on a daily basis to move yourself closer towards your goal.

Positive and constructive ideas need to be put in place so you have the best chance for success in a timeframe.

Once you start, it is amazing how many things you can think of, such as physical, mental, logistical, financial and other issues, that will need to be addressed. All should have related deadlines, but create some slack in there just in case there's a problem (injury, work or family issues, etc). It's important that you write it all down. You can make it as detailed or high level as you like depending on the type of person you are and what you are hoping to achieve. I was very ambitious and liked the detail, but that's not for everybody.

After you have created your plan and you have started on the path towards your goal, then you ought to assess yourself against the plan on a regular basis to check progress. If you find yourself slipping behind you might want to take action and rejig the plan. However, remember, if you aren't enjoying it or it's taking the fun out of your climbing then readjust and start again.

For example, I am going on a surfing trip to Indonesia in six months' time and my goal is to score the best barrel I have ever had, then my plan would be something like this: I need to swim five days a week. I need to surf whenever a swell hits my local spot. I need more flexibility so must stretch daily. I need the best fuel for my body and will eat accordingly. I need more cardiovascular fitness in my upper body so will do circuit training. I will visualise daily that incredible wave I'm going to get. I need to buy an expensive new board – well, not really, but it's a good excuse. The list goes on.

When I was super keen and motivated in competitions, I would detail my plans for the next competition. I was already training hard, stretching and eating a great diet. How could I get the edge?

Desire is a big factor. If you really want to achieve something, the likelihood of success will be much higher.

Given equal abilities, I believe the person who wants it the most and has prepared the best will succeed. I had to want to win each competition that came up more than any other climber, but that's easier said than done. If you want to win your local competition or in your own national competition it's easy to see why you want victory. Why then did I want to win the next competition which might be in Spain, France or Germany more than anyone else?

I would think up ideas, some of them very random, as part of my plan to win and why I wanted victory more than anyone. I thought of ideas and would write them down. Sometimes I would wake up in the night with another idea and think, 'That's a good one, I'll put that one down.' Eventually, I would have a list of why it was so important to win that competition. I could then read the list thereby reinforcing it in my mind. For example, I have a competition coming up in Spain.

Reasons for me wanting to win that competition more than any other climber include the following:

- I LOVE SPAIN AS A COUNTRY
- I HAVE GREAT FRIENDS THERE WHO HAVE COME TO WATCH ME
- I HAVE A SPANISH SPONSOR
- SPANISH FOOD IS GREAT
- I HAVE TRAINED HARDER THAN ANY ONE ELSE
- I ENJOY MY WIN WITH A CELEBRATION NIGHT OUT
- I NEED THE PRIZE MONEY FOR A NEW CAR
- I NEED THE RANKING POINTS
- ...

The other important thing you have to do is prepare yourself for all the problems and distractions that might arise.

This is best done well in advance. In competitions, for example, you need to be prepared for the crowd, ready to climb when your name is called. There are so many distractions and they need to be addressed early so you know how you're going to react. If you have prepared yourself early and inhibited all those negative thoughts and distractions you will be able to focus and concentrate more clearly on your climbing.

The first competition I won was in France. I was living in Germany at the time and had just blown the engine on my motorbike. There was a competition coming up and the prize money would be enough to buy a new bike. I had to go. All I could think about was winning the competition and buying a bike. I had desire, a goal and had made a plan. As it was a long drive from Germany, my plan was to get a good friend, Uli, to do the driving for me. I planned to arrive a couple of days early so as to be nice and fresh for the climbing.

The drive went well and we checked in to a nice-looking hotel. We went downstairs to dinner where my friend took a particular liking to the beautiful French waitress. This was where my plan started to fall apart.

I went to bed early, leaving Uli drinking at the bar, downing shots and chatting up the waitress. At about 2 a.m., Uli burst into the bedroom, completely drunk and larking about with the waitress. Needless to say, I wasn't too impressed and told him to go somewhere else. He went outside then staggered back in just a few minutes later asking for my car keys. Not really thinking, I passed them to him. The next thing I hear are wheelspins as he drives my car away. I never imagined he would drive the car being that drunk. I hardly slept a wink after that. Thankfully, Uli returned with my car unscathed in the morning. I was so grateful that the competition was not for another two days, so I had a day to recover and a good night's sleep to look forward to. We went into town to locate where the competition was to be held, but could find nothing. I went to the visitors' centre; again they knew nothing of a climbing competition. They kindly let

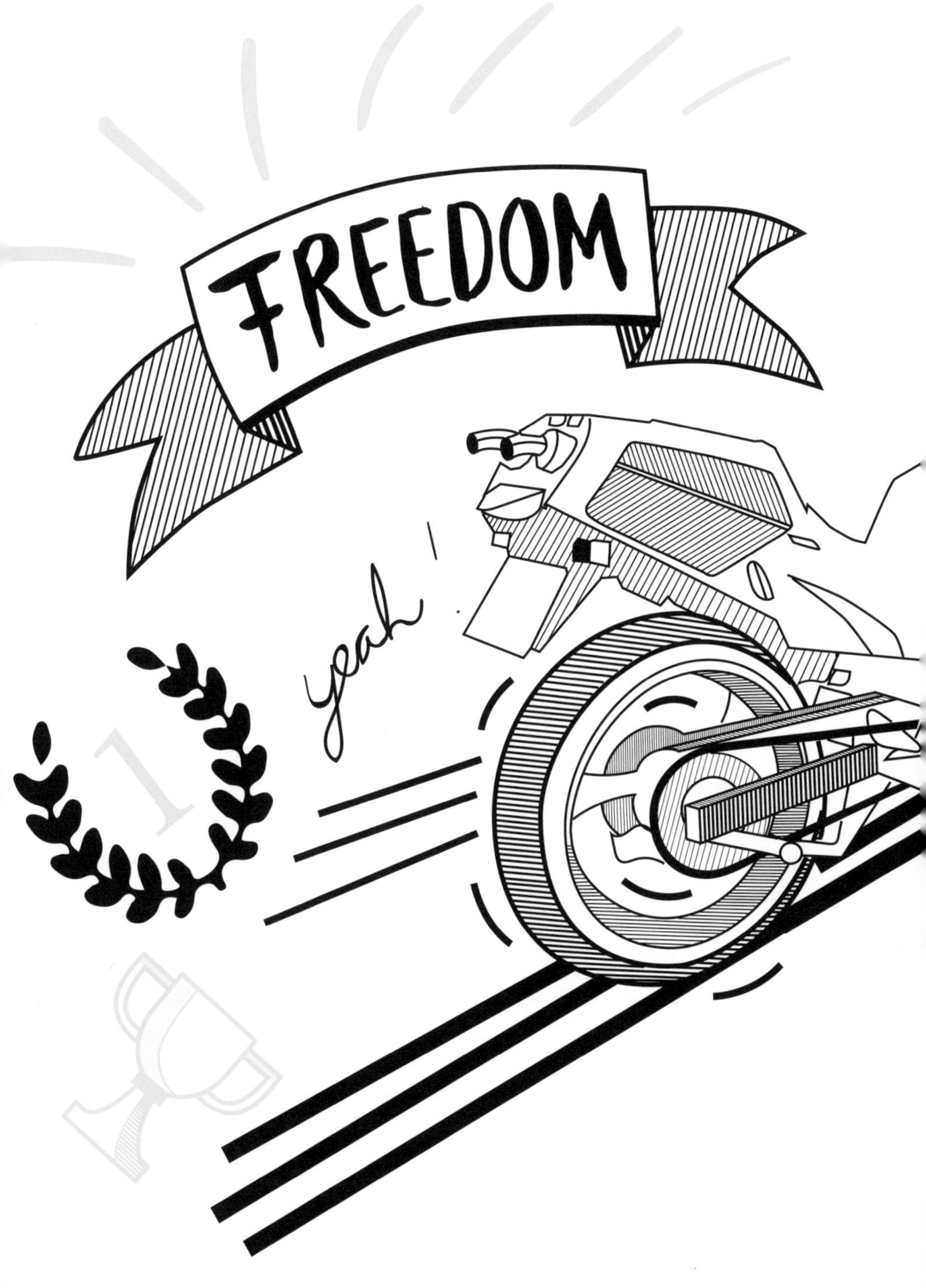
FREEDOM
yeah!
1

me use their phone to speak to the organisers. It was then I realised I had gone to the wrong place! The actual competition was five hours' further driving to the south. I was then really stressed. Uli drove at breakneck speed, getting me to the competition in the late afternoon. It had been an epic nightmare, but finally I was there. A Mike Tyson quote springs to mind here: 'Everyone has a plan until they get punched in the mouth.' Thankfully the climbing went much better for me and I won the competition. The moral of the story? Okay, my plan didn't go perfectly, but I made a big effort to make a plan and I did eventually win the competition. Two days later, I was back in Germany and the proud owner of a Yamaha TZR crotch rocket. I should add, a month after that I was the ashamed owner of a large speeding fine and in hiding from the police!

I was a professional climber and one of the highest paid for around twenty years. I had a lot of sponsors and each year I would meet with the different companies. We would discuss the budgets and my sponsorship deals for the next year. The meetings would take around an hour. That hour was critical for me, as it determined my salary for the next year. I put the techniques I used for climbing, like goal setting, making a plan and visualisation, to use in preparation for the meetings. I had to convince myself that I was absolutely worth the money I was asking for. It wasn't that easy to do because really I would think to myself, 'I can't believe they are paying me all that money just so I can go to the United States and climb for six months!'

I had to come up with as many ideas as possible of things I could offer them. I would write lists of ideas over a period of weeks. Whenever I thought of something new I would write it down, even if it was random. When it came to the time for each of the meetings, I had visualised all the potential problems and I was just raring to go. I felt I had more control in the meetings and could direct things, offering my sponsors one thing after another that I would do for them. I had it all planned out.

If you want something, that's a goal. Making a plan of how you're best going to achieve it won't guarantee it, but you're going to have a better chance. If you fail to plan then you plan to fail.

MY PLAN

LESSON

DIARY

Keeping a climbing diary is not only a great way of retaining memories, it's an extremely useful device to reinforce great climbing days and to keep you positive.

Writing memories down in detail is the best way of making sure that you retain and don't forget each positive experience and the circumstances around them. On a regular basis, you should re-read your diary to help maintain your positivity and confidence about your climbing.

Lanny Bassham's principle of reinforcements states:

'The more you think about, talk about and write about something happening, the more you improve the probability of that thing happening.'

That is the reason you need to keep a diary. Write it down, think about it and visualise and bank that great day climbing you just had.

What you write in your diary is of critical importance, as it needs to be used for positive reinforcement. I'm sure you have figured it out by now: there must be no negatives when you write down what you have done during the day. Whatever has happened in your day's climbing, you must figure out how to see the best things and a positive side to that day's climbing.

Obviously, not every day you go climbing is going to be a great one. Sometimes things just seem to be stacked up against you. The conditions might be bad, you get a split finger or your muscles are just super fatigued from your last climb.

Find something good that happened in that day's climbing no matter how small and write that down and leave the bad stuff out.

The idea is that later on you can open your diary on any page, read what you did and that page will be a positive reinforcement. If you're about to go for your hardest redpoint or difficult boulder problem you will be nervous and apprehensive. You can then pick up your diary, flick through it and look at all the great days' climbing you've had. This will lower your anxiety level and improve your mind.

Adam Ondra talks later about his final thoughts before doing something very hard. He picks out a particular day, move or route where he was climbing really well. He visualises that, thereby boosting his confidence. He then takes those thoughts into the climb. It is exactly the same principle as I'm trying to explain here, except I am saying write it down as well as think about it.

When I was competing in the late 1980s, the time in the isolation zone seemed like ages. During those times, I would get my diary out and just flip through it. It brought back so many great memories of days climbing which then put me in a wonderful place to climb.

You don't need to write very much, but if you have a really good day write more. At the bottom of what you have written for the day state your long-term goal. If your goal is to climb F8a then write down 'GOAL – I am an 8a climber.' Get this written down every day until you achieve your goal.

I recently pulled out my diary from 1990. I had put some boards in my cellar so I could train indoors at home in the dry. At that time, there were no climbing walls. A friend, Andy Pollitt, had a horizontal board we used to hang on and do footless problems and I had built one of these already. I wanted a board to do short problems with small footholds which was steep. The cellar I had is now an apartment so I had plenty of room. I angled the plywood board at about forty-five-degrees, made some holes out of wood and screwed them on. It had a kick board for your feet of about a foot. I had never seen one anywhere else or heard of one. The first forty-five-degree training board was born. It is very similar to Alex Megos' Mega board in Café Kraft nearly thirty years later. Every gym seems to have one now with people going back to wood holds.

■ ▪ ■

This is the diary entry which shows the creation of the forty-five-degree board:

Monday 8 January 1990

'Went looking for dry rock, but all was wet and not drying. Put left board on and did punchbag. Training for two hours with Zippy [Mark Pretty] did some good linking. Felt stronger than yesterday. I must put numbers on the problems and write them down before I forget. Felt strong and had a good session. Medium workout, but had to stop early as felt wrist starting to hurt on hangs.

   GOAL: I am the 1990 ASCI and World Cup Champion.'

I did not win the World Cup, as later that year I changed my direction and decided to focus on new routes, doing the first ascent of *Liquid Ambar*, the world's first F8c+. I was, however, number one in the ASCI rankings, which was a pick of the most prestigious, largest competitions with the highest prize money.

MUHAMMAD ALI

'DO NOT COUNT THE DAYS, MAKE THE DAYS COUNT!'

14 Thursday

Abbed down Martyrs took
it. out Then led it
ripping £166 ~~ascent on~~
~~washed~~ if Jelly role
brilliant.. Then led ~~pepper~~
urr-spire.

15 Friday

Dear Diary: soloed
right wall down ivy septchai
left wall foil, memory
lane and cenotab corner
went back to cafe then
bolderd a Fachwen toyed
shorters overhang did
it in two parts.

VISUALISATION

Chris Sharma

© Hannes Huch

We know that your unconscious will follow whatever your conscious mind is thinking. If it's thinking something positive, it cannot at the same time think of something negative.

We need to get your self-image (the way you think about yourself) in a great place. You don't want to be overconfident and you need to be realistic about what you are about to do. There clearly needs to be a balance. Visualisation is without doubt the most widely used psychological tool used before and during any sort of sporting activity. Literally every top climber I have spoken to uses visualisation.

Visualisation has probably been used for thousands of years. I can imagine cavemen dozing in their caves thinking about how they were going to spear their next mammoth. If they were picturing that hunting scenario and how they were going to go about it in their head, then that was visualisation. There are some great advantages to using visualisation over going to the crag. You don't have to drive there, it doesn't wear your skin down, you can't get injured, you don't fall off and so on. You will get the greatest benefits from visualisation if your mind is relaxed in a type of meditation.

Good times to visualise your performance would be just before you go to sleep, shortly after waking up or relaxing on the sofa.

There are a few ways you can visualise climbing. The first and most common way, **kinaesthetic imagery**, is to feel yourself doing movement. The second way, **external perspective imagery**, is when you watch yourself doing the climb from a distance. The third way is called **internal perspective imagery**, which is what you would see when you execute moves, such as your hand moving on to a hold.

When you visualise something your brain gets loaded up and runs with all the processes that prepare the muscles to make the thing you're thinking about happen. So when you imagine a move and do a move, everything is exactly the same apart from the last little bit

Alex Megos
visualising a
boulder problem

© Hannes Huch

which would be the impulses sent down the spinal cord, which would make your muscles work. When you're practising imagery, it's the same except your muscles don't fire to the same extent. You will not get any strength gain, but there may be some leakage of impulses. Dreaming is one of the most powerful forms of imagery. That's why sometimes your muscles will twitch and you might move while you are dreaming. That twitch is the leakage down the nervous system into the muscles.

Visualisation is a link between conscious words or thoughts in your head and movement.

When you visualise a move in your brain, it is then able to instruct your muscles to perform the movement.

If you're trying to perform movements that are very technical, the precise shape and form of the movement has to be perfect. Take gymnastics: in order to perform, your body has to be in the precise position, the right shape; everything has to be exact. External perspective imagery is very powerful for that, and highly technical climbing moves are similar.

Using external perspective imagery coupled with how it will feel (kinaesthetic imagery) is probably the most powerful imagery to use for technical movement.

Most of the time on routes when moves are not quite so technical, perhaps internal perspective imagery might work better, i.e. what you would see when you make the moves. You could do internal perspective imagery to get an idea and then think, 'Okay, now let's feel what it's like to do the moves' by using kinaesthetic imagery. Mixing the two can be quite powerful and helpful. Some people find one works better than the other. There are no hard and fast rules, so find what works for you.

Using external perspective imagery is typically associated with competitiveness. If you are in a competition and use an external perspective image of you climbing it could heighten your competitive drive. You are visualising it as the spectators would see it and as the opposition sees it. You are watching yourself and thinking, 'That's me and I'm going to beat them.'

It's important to understand the differences involved in imagery, and they are all potentially useful in different circumstances. You need to experiment to find out what works best for you. However, kinaesthetic imagery will always be important because that's how it feels. It will always add value.

When using imagery make it as realistic as you possibly can.

Picture in your head the whole process from tying into the rope to squeaking your boots at the bottom. Then do every move, feel the texture of the rock, clip the bolts, chalk up, get pumped, recover, shout for slack, fight your way through some of the moves, flow through others; it's important to visualise all the possible situations and problems which might occur.

In high-pressure, stressful environments visualisation is a great way for calming yourself down.

If you can lower your anxiety, you reduce the pressure. One way to do this is by visualising doing whatever you're stressed about well. I used to find it hard to sleep if I was going for a big on-sight or red-point the following day. I was too anxious and excited. To lower my anxiety level, I would repeatedly visualise myself doing the climb and topping out. Before I knew it my anxiety level would drop and I would get to sleep. If you ever have problems sleeping because you are worried about a particular challenge, picture that thing going smoothly and turning out well. You'll be asleep before you know it.

I asked Alex Honnold how he prepared for something challenging and he said:

'Particularly, if it's solo and climbing ropeless, then I'll think through what it feels like to be in certain positions because some kinds of movement are

ALEX HONNOLD + PROFESSIONAL ADVENTURE ROCK CLIMBER + SOLO OF HALF DOME IN ONE HOUR TWENTY-TWO MINUTES ON MAY 2012 + SOLO OF YOSEMITE TRIPLE CROWN – AN EIGHTEEN-HOUR FIFTY-MINUTE LINK-UP OF MOUNT WATKINS, *THE NOSE* AND THE REGULAR NORTH-WEST FACE OF HALF DOME + FIRST CLIMBER TO FREE SOLO YOSEMITE'S 914-METRE EL CAPITAN WALL

insecure and so they're kind of scarier than other types of moves. It is important to me to think through how I'll feel when I'm up there, so when I'm doing it I'm not suddenly like "Oh my God, this is really scary!" I know that it's supposed to be scary. I know what it feels like and I just do it.'

Regarding Alex's visualisation, he has brought another dimension into his imagery because he is bringing in how it feels not only physically, but emotionally. The more multidimensional you make imagery the more powerful it is. It's clear that he is dealing with his anxiety and not suppressing it.

To prepare for a redpoint, attempt to visualise absolutely all of it right up to clipping the chain and lowering off. Even if parts of the climb are easy, don't underestimate them and do it all. I believe a lot of routes are blown with people falling off the top on easy ground just because they have underestimated the pressure and not visualised the route all the way to the top. If you are attempting an on-sight you can still look at the climb, imagining where the difficult moves might be, and imagine the feeling of climbing it.

When I was competing, you had two minutes to observe the route before you climbed. After I had tied on, I would first look at the climb and use internal imagery combined with kinaesthetic imagery to feel myself doing the route, looking for holds, thinking where I might rest and where I thought the climb would present problems. Even if it looked desperate I would on-sight it in my head. Then, I would externally visualise it watching myself from a distance doing the climb, thereby visualising it both ways. Holding that picture, I would step on and just concentrate on executing the moves correctly.

Keeping that positive thought and then going straight into the climb your conscious mind is going from one positive thought to the next, allowing no space for negativity.

It's important to pick up possible problems and scenarios which could get in the way of the thing you are trying to achieve. If you're planning a trip to do a route or have a competition coming up that is important to you I would definitely start by visualising and picturing all the potential problems. You need to start a few weeks before the event. It might seem a strange way to go about things, but research shows it is best to be pessimistic at first, looking for negatives and then working out how to overcome them. Once those obstacles are inhibited in your head you can move forward to think more positively when the event comes around. Using visualisation is the best way to achieve this, as you will see in the competition section where Kilian Fischhuber talks about doing exactly this, weeks in advance of a competition. He visualises the emotions the pressure creates, the crowd, the journalists, so when it comes to the event he is ready. He has six overall climbing world cups which means he is very powerful mentally. Having that much success you wouldn't have thought he starts his mental preparation inhibiting negatives, but he does using visualisation.

Visualisation is fantastic for memorising and practising moves.

It can boost confidence because you're not falling when picturing yourself climbing. It's also good for capturing how you think you will feel emotionally in potentially stressful situations. If these are rehearsed in your mind you can only come out stronger.

━ ∎ ━

MUHAMMAD ALI

'IF YOUR DREAMS DON'T SCARE YOU, THEY ARE NOT BIG ENOUGH.'

'FOR SURE, I DO VISUALISE. WHEN YOU ARE OBSESSING OVER A CLIMB AND THINKING ABOUT IT. JUST HOW EPIC THE MOVES WERE. TALKING ABOUT IT WITH YOUR BUDDY AND JUST GOING THROUGH THE MOVES IN YOUR HEAD. THERE'S A POINT THOUGH WHEN YOU TRY A ROUTE SO MANY TIMES THAT YOU KNOW IT LIKE THE BACK OF YOUR HAND, WHEN YOU TRY SOMETHING SO MUCH IT GETS INGRAINED IN YOU. SOMETIMES I'LL VISUALISE THINGS BEFORE I GO TO BED, BUT BEYOND THAT WHEN I'VE FALLEN TWENTY TIMES OFF THE SAME ROUTE IN SOME WAYS YOU JUST NEED TO CLEAR YOUR MIND AND GO THERE WITH AN OPEN MIND AND JUST GO CLIMBING. IT MIGHT SOUND NEGATIVE, BUT I ACCEPT AND CONFRONT FAILURE BEFOREHAND, SO WHATEVER HAPPENS I'M JUST GONNA GO AND HAVE FUN AND TRY MY BEST.'

CHRIS SHARMA

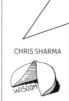

'ON REDPOINT, WHEN I WORK ON A ROUTE, FOR EXAMPLE, I WILL CLIMB THE SECTIONS AND MEMORISE HOW I FEEL. THE THING IS, BECAUSE I AM GOING BOLT TO BOLT THE ROUTE FEELS EASY. I VISUALISE HOW I FEEL WHEN I GO BOLT TO BOLT THEN IN THE END I PICTURE MYSELF CLIMBING IT AND FEELING HOW I FELT GOING BOLT TO BOLT IN EVERY SECTION. SO I WOULD FEEL TOTALLY FRESH EVEN FROM THE LAST BOLT TO THE ANCHOR. AFTER THAT, I JUST PUT IT ALL IN ONE CLIMB AND TELL MYSELF THAT'S HOW I WILL BE FEELING WHEN COMING FROM THE GROUND.'

ALEX MEGOS

ANTI-GOALS

We have covered the conscious mind, the unconscious mind and your self-image. The key is to get these three things working together in harmony. Anti-goals and ironic effect can really get in the way of this.

You need your conscious mind thinking positively and inhibiting negativity. You need a strong self-image thinking, 'I perform great in this situation.' These will allow your unconscious mind (your climbing skills) to perform to its optimum.

It is the same for all sport: great skills with a confident, conscious mind thinking positively and with a strong self-image like 'I always perform great in the final.' You want to perform to the maximum of your ability at any given time. Nobody can ask for more than that. It's what I would call a winning performance.

Your goal is to get the balance of these three things working together at the same time, which I call climbing in the 'flow state of mind'.

It is not easy to get the balance of these three things right when you throw in things like pressure, anxiety, fear of failure, prize money, an audience, a new redpoint difficulty or the first time you have on-sighted a particular grade.

I want to talk a little bit about goals and anti-goals. When this is understood I think it is very helpful. A goal is something you are attracted to and that you want to achieve. For instance, I want to do this boulder problem; I want to go to Spain and climb F9c; I want to win the World Cup in both bouldering and leading competition. An anti-goal is a thing that you want to get away from. Examples of these are: I don't want to get nervous in the bouldering competition; I'm not going to fall off the mantel on the last move of the boulder problem; I don't want to fail on that 9c as it's coming into summer and it won't

be in condition again until the winter. Anti-goals have a 'not' or 'don't' word in them and psychologically they are very different from a goal.

A goal is an attractive state creating an image in your mind of where you are trying to get to. It's like a light and you aim for it. An anti-goal is something you are trying to escape from. It's something you don't want. Anywhere but there is fine as long as you get away from the anti-goal. When your mind pictures an anti-goal, it doesn't tell you what to do, only what not to do.

A second characteristic of anti-goals is that they are associated with something called ironic effects. Everybody will have experienced ironic effect. It's when you do the one thing that you don't want to do. It's like that time when you think, 'Don't do that, don't do that', and then you do it. I had a classic one recently while taking the dogs out. I had a short chat with an elderly lady who then walked off to my left. I waited for her to get some distance away before I threw a heavy ball on a rope for the dogs. As the lady walked away, I was repeatedly thinking to myself, 'Don't throw it left, whatever you do, don't throw it left.' That anti-goal was my focus. When I threw the ball, you guessed it, I threw it left and nearly took the lady's head off! Thankfully it missed, but it was very embarrassing.

'CONTROL WRITING AND TALKING, NEVER TALK FAILURE, REMEMBER GOOD. TAKE SOMETHING YOU'RE POOR AT AND MAKE IT YOUR BEST ATTRIBUTE.'

BRUCE LEE

The best understanding of why ironic effect happens is when we're trying to achieve a goal. There are two processes that occur in tandem. One is conscious process, that is your brain seeks out information that is relative to the goal. It looks for things in the environment that can help you achieve what you're trying to do. When it recognises them it processes them and selectively attends to them and works out how you can use them. The other process is an unconscious process which tends to look for things that will mess up what you're trying to achieve. It looks for problems, obstacles and difficulties.

In normal life, these processes happen in an orderly fashion. One part of your mind which is trying to achieve the goal is conscious, which requires concentration and effort. The anti-goal is unconscious so it just sits there waiting to see if there are some potential hazards coming your way. Because it's an unconscious process it uses no mental resource. Under normal circumstances, you can control and coordinate both together. Things will come up, your mind will attend to one thing then the next thing and so on. However, when you get stressed or anxious you get depleted resources, like when you are tired or pumped out of your brain at the top of the pitch. Then the goal part of your brain finds it harder to do the conscious searching and the disruptive process anti-goal starts to take over. It finds those bad things.

Under pressure, you're much more likely to create ironic effect.

It works something like this: close your eyes, don't think of a red bus and of course you think of the red bus. The only way your brain can access the anti-goal is to identify it first. Then, as you process the anti-goal your brain goes, 'That's the thing I don't want to think about.' In the heat of the moment or under pressure that's when you make mistakes.

It is critical that if you think of a 'don't' then you need to replace it very quickly with a positive goal thought.

You need to be very aware of anti-goals, as they're not good things. Avoid at all costs self-talk using 'don't' and 'not' while doing the thing you are trying to achieve. 'Yes' is a good word to use. Try to empty your mind and think of a positive goal so you can focus on just one thing. Your mind must be a flow from one positive thought into the next one. Make sure it's a positive one, otherwise under pressure an anti-goal is likely to fill the gap.

Your self-image has to be like a rock. Thoughts like, 'I normally top out after I get through the crux. As soon as I figure out the moves of a boulder problem I send it. It's not a problem if I get pumped, I can shake out anywhere. I'm good, I'm fast, this is my time, I'm strong.'

Your performance on the rock will be directed by the mental thoughts and images you create.

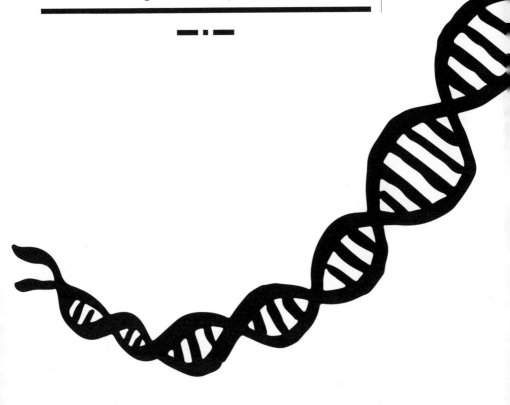

FLOW

Alex Megos

© Hannes Huch

'THE BEST MOMENTS IN OUR LIVES ARE NOT THE PASSIVE, RECEPTIVE, RELAXING TIMES. THE BEST MOMENTS USUALLY OCCUR IF A PERSON'S BODY OR MIND IS STRETCHED TO ITS LIMITS IN A VOLUNTARY EFFORT TO ACCOMPLISH SOME-THING DIFFICULT AND WORTHWHILE.'

MIHALY CSIKSZENT-MIHALYI

WISDOM

Mihaly was a pioneer in the study of the state of consciousness he called 'flow'. When the challenge and the skill are perfectly balanced, Mihaly argued it's possible to enter 'flow state' or 'flow state of mind'. There are no conscious thoughts. There is only engagement with the environment and doing.

Having your mind focused completely in the present is a key factor for any optimum performance.

In the 'flow state of mind', 'in the zone', 'in the moment' or 'state of flow' are the different terminologies for being completely immersed, fully focused and totally absorbed in something you're trying to achieve. The sensations you would typically feel while in this flow state of mind would be strength, focus, unselfconsciousness – everything seems to be effortless and you kind of forget yourself. It's possible to enter this state while doing different activities.

The key is that you're completely mentally absorbed in the activity that you're doing.

Being in that flow state of mind involves the whole aspect of the activity you are pursuing. For instance, imagine for a moment that you might be an archer. You pull back the bow, release the arrow and hit the bullseye. You do it again and again, maintaining that flow state of mind as you load the bow and do all the things involved before you release the arrow again. The archer might be in this flow state of mind for half an hour or so.

In climbing terms, you might be trying a boulder problem. You are happily working out the moves, then linking pieces together. Maybe you fall a couple of times and then send it.

In this flow state of mind, you have absolutely inhibited all distractions (hunger, pain, cold, time, fear, etc). Your mind is a hundred per cent focused on the activity at hand.

That whole experience could have been in the flow state of mind. It doesn't necessarily mean success or failure, it's more a total absorption in the activity. For peak performance, you need to get yourself into that flow state of mind prior to your climbing. It is only possible to enter a flow state of mind if you are using all of your mental capacity.

Another climbing example would be where you have been failing on a particular climb. Then one day you tie in and everything feels right. You feel in control, confident and only focused on one thing:

'THE SECRET OF HEALTH FOR BOTH MIND AND BODY IS NOT TO MOURN FOR THE PAST, WORRY ABOUT THE FUTURE OR ANTICIPATE TROUBLES, BUT TO LIVE IN THE PRESENT MOMENT WISELY AND EARNESTLY.'

BUDDHA

WISDOM

the moves in front of you. As you climb you feel strong, your foot-work feels precise and you're hitting each hold perfectly. You are completely unaware of people shouting encouragement, focusing completely on the next move in front of you. You're not thinking of what you've just climbed or the moves coming up. Time just seems to stand still. The next thing you know you're at the belay. It might feel effortless, almost spiritual. You've just had a peak experience. You have just climbed in the flow state of mind.

As you have focused all your energy on your chosen goal, your physical energy simply goes in that direction.

As you climb nothing else matters. Your brain's inputs are devoted to one activity, hence the feeling that time stands still. You don't feel the pain in your forearms or fingertips. Negative thoughts don't enter your head. Your mind is just so focused on the climb it can't focus on anything else. This flow state of mind experience only arrives after intense, engaged focus, where you're able to block out all things not relevant to the thing you are trying to achieve.

In this state, your conscious mind and self-image are in perfect harmony and you are climbing at your limit.

You do not want to be dwelling on things which have happened before, possibly negative, worrying about the future and what the outcome might be. Staying committed to focusing on the present will improve your concentration, calmness, clarity and give you a positive frame of mind interconnected to the moment and what you're trying to achieve. If you're not in the moment then it's not possible to be totally committed and connected.

When you are focused, being completely committed and concentrated on what's in front of you is what makes sport and in our case climbing so addictive. All life's other chores and troubles are put on hold. Nothing is of importance at that moment in time apart from the next move.

Here are some thoughts on how to get yourself into this place of 'being in the present', before you're about to climb. The thing you are about to do has to be challenging because if it is not challenging it is not going to require your full concentration.

The more you concentrate on a task and inhibit distractions the better. Strong focus is required.

Be aware of what is around you. Take everything in: the clouds, the weather. It doesn't matter too much what it is, just try and feel a presence, of being there.

Think about the reason you are there; it's where you want to be.

The climb you are about to try is what you want to do. Start to focus on what you are about to attempt.

Narrow your attention right down to what is required. Inhibit things you don't need and that might distract you. Find your process goal.

Then attend to and selectively focus on things you need to make the climb. That is executing the moves as precisely and efficiently as possible. Remember the more you can narrow and centre your focus, the better your concentration. Focus and calmness is what you are looking for.

ALEX MEGOS

'When I climb it feels like I'm in a bubble; everything feels slowed down. Sometimes when I'm deciding which way to do a move in my head, working it out a lot of the time it feels like I'm taking ages. Then I see it on video and it all happens in a split second.'

Alex is climbing in the present. He is in the zone and focusing on the next move.

In fact, all the top climbers I've spoken to say they don't really think about anything when they climb. The reason is that their mind is in the present state.

Many psychologists argue that when you perform brilliantly you are likely to be in that state of mind. However, there is probably one emotional state which is stronger, perhaps the strongest of all; unfortunately it's probably not attainable consistently. You might just have heard stories where extraordinary feats of strength are shown in super-extreme conditions like this one.

In 1988, Vietnam vets Tiny and Steve were working on a site in Hawaii. Tiny was on the ground while Steve transported things using his helicopter, until he experienced mechanical problems. The helicopter crashed in a ditch. Tiny and his fellow workers ran to the helicopter and found Steve with his leg trapped under the chopper. That was when Tiny managed to do a superhuman thing. He lifted the crashed helicopter enough to help free his buddy. Steve escaped the crash with minor injuries.

In normal circumstances, the feat would not be possible. Tiny probably did not look at the helicopter and think, 'Here is a challenge, I shall empty my mind of all thought.' More likely he would be thinking, 'I must save Steve.' Fear would be his overwhelming thought and move him to do a superhuman feat. No matter how hard you try when you're climbing, you virtually never totally expend all your energy. Sportsmen or women at the very top of their game are likely to get the closest. When Tiny lifted the helicopter, he got there.

He's probably reached one hundred per cent and it's not done free of fear. It is more likely done with complete fear. That fear would produce a huge amount of adrenaline, also known as epinephrine, the fight hormone.

Therefore, it is not strictly true that an open mind, focused strictly on the present, is best.

Somewhere there needs to be some element of fear. That fear must be controlled and is the force behind the performance.

It is likely that it's not possible to obtain optimum performance without an element of fear, as it is just so powerful. Most of the time fear can be disruptive, as it is very hard to control, but when controlled it is an amazing force.

The flow state of mind is the one to aim for, although it is worth noting the other level above that.

Some of the routes done on gritstone, which is our local rock in Sheffield, are really dangerous. It is not ethical to place bolts or pitons, therefore routes have to be either soloed or done on natural protection. Quite a number of people regularly risk their lives, being paralysed or breaking bones. It is always absolutely amazing to me that there are not more accidents. Really it is just incredible. I believe it's possible that fear is the one thing that has resulted in so few people getting hurt as they perform, for them, superhuman feats.

A final thought on the matter: risk and fear is everything. Do not try to get rid of them, they are very important. Learn to live with them and use them, don't suppress them and get rid of them.

'When I feel I'm climbing my best I'm just purely in the moment responding to the circumstances where you feel just super in the present. That's the part with all that aspect of climbing being our identity. All that stuff can be a hindrance to success; to be able to let go of all that is the big paradox.
I think climbing is the best way to stay in the present, concentrate on what you're doing then you can't be focused on anything else. That's why to climb is pretty cool; it forces you to concentrate and if your mind strays you're going to fall.'

CHRIS SHARMA

OPTIMISM

For all great performances in sport you need a positive attitude. A good positive attitude is created by optimism. Optimism and a positive attitude will always work in your favour.

While the above is true, it is important to remember that optimism has to be earned. You can't just be optimistic about something without first knowing what exactly is involved in the thing you're trying to do. For instance, if I had a trip coming up to Fontainebleau in two months' time and think to myself optimistically, 'I will do all the problems I try and everything is going to go great', it doesn't really have any factual backing. Far better to think, 'I have a trip coming up. In order to succeed I need to train a little harder, work on my flexibility, stop going to that nightclub for a month', and so on. It would also be wise to imagine what it is going to be like when you finally get there. How would you react if the conditions were not perfect? What if you split a fingertip on the first day? Things like this need to be thought out so you know how you are going to react.

Once you have gone through all the things you imagine could go wrong and worked out solutions to those potential issues, then it is possible to be optimistic.

BRUCE LEE

WISDOM

'OPTIMISM IS A FAITH THAT LEADS TO SUCCESS.'

Chris Sharma
being optimistic

© Ricardo
Giancola

Patience is a very important asset. Although patience and optimism are different things, I feel that being a little optimistic can help with your patience. For instance, you are bouldering in Fontainebleau and it is not going as well as you had hoped. Perhaps conditions are not great, your skin is thin or you just feel weak from the previous day's climbing. Be optimistic and patient, tell yourself things like 'When it cools down I should get it' or 'After a rest today I'm going to send it.' Those positive thoughts create a little optimism and will enable you to be more patient.

It is not possible to be optimistic and pessimistic about the same thing.

Acknowledge this and if you feel pessimistic try and replace it with some optimism. Pessimism creates negativity and blunts the tools needed for success. It must be eliminated from your thoughts. The choice is yours. Simply choose the positive, which is optimism.

A few years ago, I went surfing in Nicaragua. It was a particularly difficult wave for me to surf. Choosing the wrong wave would result in a severe beating and hold-down – not nice. The result was long waits for the right wave – particularly challenging for me and my tendency to be impatient. The impatience created thoughts in my mind like 'I'm having a bad session. Why are no waves coming to me?' This resulted in negativity. I realised this and that I had to turn it around. The Bruce Lee quote 'Optimism is a faith that leads to success' was my mantra. I sat in the water and patiently waited, repeating the mantra. Eventually, I got some great waves and managed to avoid too many beatings on the extremely shallow beach break.

'Good things come to those who wait ... '

... is a great thought to have and a classic example of patience and optimism.

— ∎ —

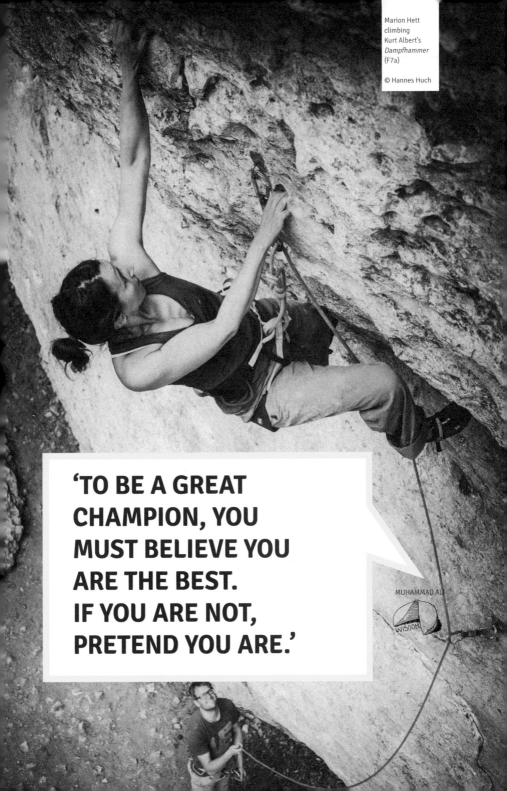

Marion Hett
climbing
Kurt Albert's
Dampfhammer
(F7a)

© Hannes Huch

'TO BE A GREAT
CHAMPION, YOU
MUST BELIEVE YOU
ARE THE BEST.
IF YOU ARE NOT,
PRETEND YOU ARE.'

MUHAMMAD ALI

WISDOM

TALKING YOURSELF UP

The way you talk and what you talk about will in-fluence your performance.

For instance, you are about to try a route that your friend has just on-sighted. You are just about to climb when he points out the route has just gone into the sun. Then he tells you that the crux is going to be really hard, as it involves a sequence of moves on slopers: 'Those slopers are going to be impossible to hold in the sun.'

We know from conscious processing and iconic effect that your conscious mind now pictures sloping holds in full sun which are impossible to hold. To eliminate those bad thoughts, your mind has first to picture them, process the thought and then inhibit them. If those thoughts are not eliminated they will more likely move your unconscious to perform in a way that is detrimental. Listening to your friend has just made your on-sight much harder.

You need to be around people who are talking positively.

If somebody has just climbed well they will be buzzing. You want some of that positive energy. Being excited for that person, congratulating them and talking about how well they climbed will give you a lift and create great pictures for your mind. Being around someone after they have just fallen off the last move of a long-term project will do you no good at all. My advice is to stay well away. Talk to them on the drive home, but don't let their downer rub off on you.

I remember one competition in Vienna where I walked away from a conversation too late. In those days, your high point on a lead was the last place you touched, not the last hold you held. In the semi-final there was a difficult traverse. Some climbers decided rather than attempt the traverse to jump and slap for a high point. I had completed the climb so it made no difference to me. There was a big discussion going on between some of the climbers about who had got further along the traverse but were beaten by the climbers who had just slapped for distance. It seemed wrong to me and I got involved in the discussion. In a flash, I realised it was bringing me down and I walked away immediately. I would never slap for distance as to me

'WATCH YOUR THOUGHTS BECAUSE THEY BECOME YOUR WORDS, YOUR WORDS WILL BECOME YOUR ACTIONS, YOUR ACTIONS WILL BECOME YOUR HABITS, YOUR HABITS WILL BECOME YOUR CHARACTER AND YOUR CHARACTER WILL DETERMINE YOUR FUTURE.'

HINDU

it felt like cheating. Along came the final. I was the last climber out. It was going pretty well. As I neared the top I was getting really pumped and looking at a hard move. For a fraction of a second I paused; the thought flashed into my head, should I slap the distance? I had never had that thought before. It was put into my mind as a result of the conversations I had listened to earlier. That interruption put doubt in my mind and I hesitated. I went for the hold, but was unable to stick it and fell. I was joint leader with the French climber Jacky Godoffe. As they hadn't made any other routes, we just had to go again on the same route. I only rested about five minutes, which wasn't enough, and was unable to reach my high point. Jacky won the competition. I'm absolutely sure if I hadn't been involved in that conversation about slapping for distance I would have made that move and won.

Imagine how a champion would think and talk about themselves internally.

My fingers are strong, my footwork is great, I read moves quickly, I find rests anywhere, I can just keep going when I'm pumped, if I can do the moves I always complete the route, the conditions are perfect. This is a great way to talk about yourself.

In 2016, a couple of golfing friends of mine, Jonathan Smart (the caddie) and Danny Willett, won a huge tournament in the US called the Masters. It's the first major golf tournament of the year, with prize money of $1.8 million, boosted to closer to $10m with increased sponsorship, etc. It's one of the biggest ones to win.

I used to play with Jonathan, as he was in the same golf club. He introduced me to Danny and I took them both climbing one day at the Foundry Climbing Centre. We played golf a couple of times too, which was great. I went out for lunch with Jonathan and we talked about their amazing victory. After the third day they were in the top ten with only one round to go. Danny was hitting shots later that evening on the practice range. Their physiotherapist came over congratulating them. He suggested if they could get into the top five it would be a great result.

Danny and Jonathan were not too impressed, asking him if he was joking or having a laugh. They asked him politely to be on his way.

Danny was there to win. Listening to top five talk was like listening to talk of failure. Top five was not his goal; he didn't even want to entertain the thought. I just love that super-positive winning attitude.

Jerry flashing
Equinox (5.12c)

© John Bachar

REHEARSAL

We have talked about visualisation, which is the most commonly used form of rehearsal. The idea of rehearsal is being prepared for all eventualities. If your mind is in a good space when you start climbing then you are on to a winner.

Familiarising yourself with the lead-up to your performance and how you are going to feel when you actually make a start can only help. You want to be thinking, 'Yes, this is how I expected it. This is normal.' You definitely do not want to be thinking, 'Well, I didn't expect that. What's this all about?' It's important here to picture all the possible problems along with the positives.

Interestingly, when I spoke to Stefan Glowacz recently he told me how Martina Navratilova (winner of eighteen grand slam singles titles) used to prepare for tennis tournaments. She would familiarise herself with the whole area where she was due to play her next tournament. If it was Wimbledon, she would turn up two weeks before when no one was around. Martina would spend time in the changing room, rehearsing in her head the kind of feelings she might have. She would then walk out on to Centre Court familiarising herself with the surroundings so she knew exactly what to expect when the time came around for real. She made a habit of doing this for the big events she competed in. It's a fantastic plan of action. It's like a real-life rehearsal. You're making the competition yours.

Stefan said he went to Paris two weeks before Bercy, which was the biggest competition of 1990. He had a walk round the whole area familiarising himself, visualising what he was going to be up against when the time came. He didn't actually win that competition, but he put himself in a good position to do so.

On that occasion, I won. I had travelled to the south of France for a couple of weeks to train, as it was winter and the rock was wet in England. I was staying in a caravan in Buoux, but didn't really want to be there. There were few climbers around and it was quite cold. I was really motivated for the competition and I really needed this preparation. In that small, damp, cold, smelly, rented caravan I listened to the French 'Fun Radio' station where they kept promoting the competition. The radio station mentioned all the big climbers' names who would be attending – Jacky Godoffe, Jean-Baptiste Tribout, Stefan Glowacz, Marc Le Menestrel – but they never mentioned me. That wound me up something rotten. As I sat in my damp caravan I thought, 'That's my competition. I'm gonna win it and show that radio station to leave my name out!'

This is one of the things that I rehearsed to get myself in the right frame of mind to compete. I knew from previous competitions that the time I got nervous was when my name was called out and I walked out to face the audience from the isolation zone. It's the contrast from the peace and quiet backstage to suddenly going where all the action and noise is. To prepare for this, I uncoiled a rope and put it on the floor of the caravan, then I put my harness on. I sat on the edge of the bed imagining my name being called. I visualised the feelings I would be having. I then walked over to the rope; I waved and smiled at an imaginary audience again visualising it. I tied into the rope then looked up to an imaginary wall and visualised myself climbing in the competition. I did this a few times on a couple of evenings. I had rehearsed and pictured exactly how I was going to walk out in front of the audience in Paris. Anyone looking in through the caravan window would have thought I was mad!

I felt calm when the competition came round and my name was called. I knew precisely what I was going to do. I had faced my fears and worries early on. I walked across the hall, smiled and waved at the crowd, tied into the rope, looked at the route. Then, I used kinaesthetic and internal imagery of myself climbing it. I externally visualised it again and started climbing. I was absolutely ready and in my mind I had done that walk so many times before and knew what to expect. This had put me in a better position than someone who had not rehearsed it at all.

What you are looking for is lots of small advantages to get you over the line.

■ ▪ ■

PRESSURE

Pressure: it's such a big part of any sporting performance of great importance.

People often think that pressure can hinder performance. There are only two ways to look at it: one, 'I don't like pressure and am likely to buckle', or two, 'I love pressure and need it for optimum performance.' I would say that it's not possible to have a really amazing performance without pressure. You need to do it when it matters, that's the test.

The greatest performances of all time are often done under the greatest amount of pressure.

Just look at the amount of world records that are broken in the Olympic finals, particularly in sprinting where race tactics don't really involve other runners. An Olympic performer is performing for their psychological life. It's been years of training and psychologically if they fail they die. They are driven by fear, and the pressure is absolutely immense.

It is also possible to buckle under pressure. It is amazing how your personal performance can be affected so much by pressure.

It's important to understand that it is normal to feel pressure and that the adrenaline response is natural. You don't need to deny it, but rather embrace it. The important thing is not to give in to it and learn to control it.

One problem with a sportsperson's response to pressure is often trying too hard. It's quite natural in a competition or under pressure to get out of your normal routine, to rush, strain, pull too hard and tighten up. You will climb better if you just climb normally, trying as hard as you can in normal circumstances, rather than trying to force it artificially.

'WHEN THE ATHLETE IS RUNNING AS FAST AS HE CAN, HE SHOULD NOT FEEL AS THOUGH HE OUGHT TO BE RUNN-ING FASTER. OVERALL TENSION AND UNNECESSARY MUS-CULAR CONTRACTIONS ACT AS BREAKS, RE-DUCING SPEED AND DISSIPATING ENERGY.'

BRUCE LEE

To help deal with pressure situations, a little self-talk never goes amiss. Use some of your positive declaration statement. Repeat the words to yourself like 'I'm fit, I'm strong, I believe in myself, this is my time.' These positive thoughts and pictures you are creating in your mind will help lower your anxiety.

If you feel yourself tightening up under pressure a good tip is to smile.

Try it. It has the effect of relaxing your muscles. It will just relieve a little tension. Nearly all the techniques outlined in this book will help with pressure. Visualisation, improved self-image, talking yourself up, banking success, embracing fear and anxiety, inhibiting problems and narrowing your focus down to one process goal to improve your concentration.

When he's under pressure, Alex Megos says, 'I'm just going to do it.' It's simple, short and sweet and he consistently uses that thought before he pulls on.

How's this for a pressure situation? Back to my golfing pals Danny Willett and Jonathan Smart. They have played golf for three days and it's the final day. They are on the last hole and in position to win. Danny hits the perfect drive, leaving just one more shot to the green. It's a life-changing moment, even if you forget the millions of dollars of prize money involved. More than anything they want to win the Masters. Jonathan has to pick the correct club for the shot Danny is preparing to execute. Picking the wrong club could cost them victory.

Here's what Jonathan said:

'We had 175 yards to the flag which was at the front of the green. I spoke to Dan about the shot we needed. He wanted to hit a draw from the right which kind of gives the ball topspin. I thought that the risk was too high if Dan didn't hit that shot perfectly. I am not employed as a yes-man and I suggested that he hit a higher shot with more backspin. Under pressure you can't just hit shots you're comfortable with; sometimes you've got to hit the harder shot because it's the right shot. I totally knew the consequences. It wasn't about calmness, it was about making the right decision or the wrong decision. After a short discussion, we agreed what shot to make and we talked it through in detail to create a picture. Dan went through his routine and played the shot perfectly. I get goose bumps thinking about it. Before I started on tour, I thought I would be thinking of the huge amounts of prize money. Actually, it never crosses your mind. You are just trying so hard to win. If you imagine two hamsters running round on a wheel seeing who can go the longest, we are the hamster that's just not gonna stop till we collapse and there is absolutely nothing left.'

'CHAMPIONS ARE NOT MADE IN THE GYMS. CHAMPIONS ARE MADE FROM SOMETHING THEY HAVE DEEP INSIDE THEM: A DESIRE, A DREAM, A VISION.'

MUHAMMAD ALI

'I THINK THE WAY I'VE OPERATED IS JUST TALKING YOURSELF OUT OF PRESSURE. SOME OF YOUR BEST DAYS ARE LIKE, "WHAT THE HELL, LET'S JUST GO AND TRY FOR FUN." TRY AND TRICK YOURSELF INTO WAYS OF HAVING NO EXPECTATIONS, WHICH IS HARD. MY TECHNIQUE FOR GETTING THROUGH THE MENTAL BARRIERS IS JUST BANGING MY HEAD AGAINST THAT WALL UNTIL I BREAK IT DOWN AND JUST KEEP TRYING AND TRYING. BASICALLY JUST DISARM YOURSELF, JUST SURRENDER YOURSELF.

IT'S LIKE, LET'S GO CLIMBING AND CLIMB BECAUSE YOU LOVE CLIMBING AND THAT'S WHEN YOU CLIMB YOUR BEST. IT CAN BE A FRUSTRATING PROCESS. THE ONLY THING THAT I CAN SAY IS THAT BY BECOMING A PARENT THAT WHOLE PROCESS HAS BECOME EASIER BECAUSE LESS OF MY IDENTITY AND EGO ARE CAUGHT UP IN THAT. IT'S BEEN SO MUCH EASIER TO ACCESS THAT MINDSET WHEN THE MAGIC HAPPENS. SO MAYBE THE KEY IS TO HAVE BABIES!'

CHRIS SHARMA

WISDOM

FAILURE

Even if you have the strongest fingers, the strongest arms, the best footwork and strongest mental game you are not going to succeed every single time.

Even the very best have off days and fail on routes or problems they should do easily. It is a fact of life which needs to be understood and accepted.

Winners are not people who don't fail, they are people who don't quit.

If you have ever played cards you know that sometimes it's just not your day, continually getting bad cards. You might play the next day and, boom, you get all good cards and continually win.

Imagine you are holding a handful of coins above a chequered chessboard. If you drop them they will land randomly on white and

BRUCE LEE

'DON'T FEAR FAILURE. NOT FAILURE, BUT LOW AIM, IS THE CRIME. IN GREAT ATTEMPTS, IT IS GLORIOUS EVEN TO FAIL.'

black. Some might gather all in one corner, some squares may have no coins. You would not expect an even distribution of coins to result in one per square. If things are not going your way, it could just be the coins are not falling right for you.

In climbing, this might be an unexpected slip from a foot pressing too hard on a polished hold. How you react is very important. Going over your failure repeatedly in your mind is obviously bad because you're reinforcing negative thoughts. It's not a problem to reflect on a failure objectively and learn from that. Analyse it and then move on. Tell yourself, if you are not failing you are not challenging yourself enough.

It's pointless wasting energy on negative thoughts; let it go.

I remember one time surfing on the east coast of Yorkshire. It was very cold with snow on the ground. I was trying to surf a reef, which is a wave breaking over a rock slab. It's difficult as the wave is what surfers would call hollow, which means the drop on the take-off was very steep and barrelling almost immediately. I kept getting to my feet then falling off on my bottom turn, unable to get the nose of my board out of the water. It was annoying the hell out of me watching the flawless wave going into the distance with me not on it. I was not calm. Not only that, every time I got it wrong I was getting beaten up under the water, freezing my ass off with a ten-minute paddle back to where I started. I sat in the water getting more and more angry, thinking about falling off that bottom turn. Suddenly, I realised what I was doing: just reinforcing the mental picture of me falling again and again. What an idiot. I then sat on my board, closed my eyes and just visualised myself getting to my feet and making a perfect bottom turn. I did this repeatedly, calming my anger down and regaining my composure. When the next wave came, I didn't really think, I just went. I made the take-off and bottom turn without a problem, getting an absolute bomb of a ride. Beforehand, I had let my frustration and anger take over my failure, which benefited me in no way at all.

Next time you're failing on the boulder problem, getting frustrated and kicking your chalk bag or screaming at the rock when you've fallen off the last move of your project yet again, let it go, forget it.

Try to get back into creating a more positive mental picture and space where you can perform to the best of your ability. If you can't visualise yourself succeeding it will make it harder to actually succeed. I like how Ondra thinks when he is failing; he reflects in a positive way.

ADAM ONDRA

WISDOM

'MOST OF ALL, IF I FAIL I'M FRUSTRATED, BUT EVERY FAILURE IS A LESSON THAT MAKES ME THINK WHAT I DID WRONG SO I CAN COME BACK AND BE STRONGER.'

Fear of failure is not really dealing with losing, it is something quite different. It's more like you not putting yourself into the firing line because you think you are not going to do well.

More than anything else, fear of failure prevents people from reaching their full potential in all walks of life.

It's very easy to allow a fear of failure, or more accurately the consequences of failure, to take over before you even step on to the rock. Indeed, these thoughts in your head could be so strong that it stops you even attempting to reach your full potential.

'DEFEAT SIMPLY TELLS ME THAT SOMETHING IS WRONG IN MY DO-ING; IT IS A PATH LEAD-ING TO SUCCESS AND TRUTH. IT IS NOT WHAT HAPPENS IN OUR LIFE THAT IS IMPORTANT, IT IS HOW WE REACT TO WHAT HAPPENS. FAILURE IS WHAT YOUR MIND ACKNOWLEDGES.'

BRUCE LEE

The trouble with fear of failure is that sometimes it's hard to pin-point exactly what the fear is. It's pretty clear if the climber intends to do a very dangerous climb or solo something. In that situation, there is only one real fear: killing yourself. You're not exactly going, to think, 'Oh, that could be embarrassing.'

More commonly, fear of failure may relate to less serious issues. There might be all sorts of different things to be scared of. A lot of them have to do with your ego and pride. For example, thinking that you might look stupid if you fall off in front of your friends or someone you're trying to impress. You might be climbing really well, but be afraid of attempting a particular on-sight knowing that if you fail you would have blown the one chance of that on-sight flash which would be really annoying. As a result, you keep leaving the big effort for another day.

You must not let your fear of looking bad and the dent to your ego that goes with that interfere with what you're attempting to do.

Everyone suffers from this affliction without question, however great a climber or competitor they might be.

When you feel these effects and stresses try focusing and thinking about something completely different, for example where you are or the people around you. This is a situation where you need to really focus your mind on the present. Look at your surroundings perhaps and the beautiful countryside, the clouds; try and take your mind to different places. This will help shift your focus away from yourself. Once you've calmed down you can refocus and get ready to dig deep and battle.

'*First Round, First Minute* [F9b] was a good example for me on another project which went on and on and on and I just kept falling over and over and over again. It went on for over a couple of years. An interesting moment for me because I had to confront failure fully. Not just like in a competition which is one day, but I dedicated two years of my life to something. It's a strange feeling because climbing is always about progression, taking it up a step. If you fail that step you can't just skip that step. I had to accept it and move on to work another project which I had not done, which is 9b+. I almost did that route, to this day my best try. I then belayed my friend who did his project, it was the end of the day and I just thought, let's give *First Round, First Minute* a try and I did it that day. Somehow confronting failure and accepting that helped. It's a big hit to our ego and you have to accept it. I didn't think I was ever going to do it. I must have fallen fifty times off the last move. I was over it, I wasn't even enjoying it. So sometimes it's good to take a step back to solve a problem. When you get attached to the outcome then that prevents you from achieving it and you get really frustrated and fall a bunch of times.'

CHRIS SHARMA

OBSTACLES

Obstacles are often unforeseen things which might get in the way and need to be overcome so you can perform to the best of your ability.

You have to be ready for all eventualities. It is inevitable that unexpected things might happen to you on your pre-planned big day.

For instance, the conditions are perfect, you have had a rest day and feel super strong and ready to redpoint your first 7c. On the way to the cliff you get a puncture and are unable to get one of the bolts off to change the wheel and you have an epic. Is that going to spin your mind out? 'Oh no. It's not my day. I can't believe it's happening to me.' Well, you have to be ready for that. How do you react? Here are a couple of options. One option is to go to pieces believing that fate is against you and it's never going to happen. The other is to think, 'It's not a problem, I always climb better in the afternoon.'

I remember one particular competition in the late 1980s. I was waiting in the isolation zone for a semi-final. Patrick Edlinger was the next climber to go out. Patrick was one of the very first celebrity climbers, sponsored and well paid. He was very famous in France and recognised all the time by the public when he was out. He won a few competitions and was a fantastic climber, certainly one of the best in the world at the time. As they called his name to climb, he tightened his boots one more time. Then pop, his laces broke right in the middle of the boot. It was then all a bit of a panic as he tried to rearrange the laces. It completely threw him. The result was that he didn't make the semi-final. I don't know for certain, but that broken lace probably cost him a place in the final and who knows, he might have won it. I thought to myself, how would I have reacted in that situation? I realised that to perform better I needed to know instantly how I would react to something negative in order to eliminate that panic of 'Oh no, what do I do now?' This is the important bit.

If you know immediately what your reaction will be you can eliminate that space when your mind starts thinking negative thoughts. You need to go straight into a positive action.

There was nothing Patrick could have done about his broken laces.

Sometimes you just have to accept what fate throws at you.

That's your exam paper for the day, see what you can do with it.

In that situation, better to think, 'I often warm up without doing my boots up properly. I know I can climb hard moves like that. Wouldn't it be amazing if I could climb the semi-final with my boots not laced up properly. It's a great challenge, that's what I'm going to do.'

I wrote a list of all the obscure things that could possibly go wrong and next to that how I would react to each problem. For instance, I go to chalk up and I have not done my knot up properly, so my chalk bag falls to the ground. Reaction: no problem at all. On my hardest redpoints it's not possible to chalk up. I can climb my hardest problems with minimal chalk.

I know it seems extreme, but you have to think of everything. There are two climbers competing with exactly the same ability; one climber has gone to the trouble of doing the lists and getting ready for all eventualities. My money would be on that climber.

■ ∎ ■

Margo Hayes
preparing for the
obstacle of high
footholds.

© Cathy Hayes

WHAT CAN GO WRONG

LESSON

HOW TO REACT TO IT

CHOKING

Choking is when you fail to reach an expected level of performance in a pressure situation. If the failure is not one hundred per cent down to pressure, it's not choking. Choking is something that happens to absolutely everybody. For everybody it happens to it's absolutely horrendous.

Attaining peak performance is complicated at the top end of any sport. In climbing, for instance, any number of things could go wrong and your job is to get them right. Some of them are having the ap-

propriate goals, being able to concentrate, staying in the present, inhibiting stuff that is not relevant, focusing on stuff that's important, about being physically fit, warming up properly, having your body in the appropriate activation state, thinking positively about the event, the conditions, your skin, how rested your body is. Lots of things could go wrong.

Choking is very different from facing a dangerous or life-threatening situation. It is still possible to choke in a dangerous situation, and classic signs of this are trying much too hard, overgripping holds and consequently getting pumped.

Here is an example of when I choked while climbing at my first ever competition held in the Pyrenees in Troubat. We had to work a route and redpoint it the following day. When I worked the route I climbed the first groove which was about eight metres without falling or much of a struggle. I then proceeded to work the headwall, which wasn't too bad. I was quietly confident that I ought to be able to do the route.

As it was my first competition, I was inexperienced. While I waited in the isolation area for my time to climb I thought it would be best to be really relaxed and not think about the competition. In this, I was very successful and fell asleep in the sunshine! I woke up perhaps five minutes before it was my time to climb. 'Don't think about it. Just relax,' I thought to myself.

As I walked out to tie on in front of the crowd suddenly the whole thing hit me. I had so many thoughts going through my head. I completely panicked, my heart rate went up and I got a massive adrenaline rush. With a big fight, I just made it to the headwall, but then I felt completely gone. I completely choked and buckled under pressure.

Here is another example of failure which is definitely not choking, as you can't pinpoint it solely down to pressure. In this climbing situation, you might be working a route to redpoint. You are doing the last moves with ease. You attempt it from the ground, make it through the crux getting to the last move, but you fall off a very simple move you would normally do easily. I've seen it happen so many times and it's one of the most frustrating things.

Failure on this occasion could be due to a number of things. You start to think it's in the bag, as you are no longer frightened, stop concentrating and become complacent. Another possibility is you still have the fear driving the energy, but now get distracted by the prospect of success. You might start focusing on the end, thereby failing to inhibit the things that are not relevant. The only thing relevant in this case is the next move. It could be you get to a rest, shake out and switch off. As you start to climb again you don't switch on fully and you get overwhelmed by the fear or difficulty of the moves. Most common would probably be being distracted by the finish and not staying focused.

A typical cause of choking is not mentally preparing properly for a pressure situation. If you have an event or route coming up which you're anxious about, you need to start thinking about it well in advance. You need to imagine how you are going to feel and how you are going to cope with the pressure.

Try to pinpoint exactly the things you think will be stressing you and how you are going to react to them.

Try and go through those negatives so you can inhibit them early on and therefore enable you to focus clearly on what's required for you to succeed in your required task.

With experience, your climbing in normal situations will be an unconscious skill, just like walking or riding a bike. The more you climb and train, the more your skill level will improve. If you try too hard your conscious mind could override your unconscious (which are your climbing skills). Your body will tighten up and your mind will be occupied with all sorts of distractions.

You need simply to focus on what you have to do, the next move in front of you. Let the skills you've learnt do the work without you trying to take over.

It's much easier said than done when the pressure is really on. With experience and practice you will be able to lessen the likelihood of choking.

ROUTINE & FINAL THOUGHT

A routine is something specific, a practical function done in readiness for an event.

It is used by virtually every single top sportsperson. Having some sort of routine before you climb is going to help. However, it is an advanced technique which will only really help if you are very experienced. It will help your preparation and consistency to be ready both physically and mentally. It can be used all the time so that it becomes natural and not something that you have to think about. It should be second nature.

It is the trigger to get you in the optimum mindset required to get the best outcome.

I am not talking about doing things out of superstition like wearing your favourite T-shirt or crossing yourself, kissing your fingers and looking to the sky. Superstitious things are not specific practical functions. With superstitious things, like if you couldn't get hold of your favourite T-shirt or chalk bag, you would be in trouble.

My routine for a boulder problem would be: I have already cleaned my boots and I'm sitting or standing directly in front of the boulder. I would then use kinaesthetic and internal imagery combined to do the whole problem in my head, chalk up and then have my final thought, saying to myself, 'focused aggression'. I would then start to climb immediately.

A good routine comes into play when the pressure is really on. When you are so nervous it's like your body is numb and it feels like you are in a dream. It is most useful at critical times and is something to rely on. If your routine gets broken just go back to the start and do it again. A routine involves using the things required to do the activity you're pursuing. In climbing you would need things like boots, chalk bag, rope and harness. Obviously using all those things in a routine might take a long time. A climbing routine for routes might be: you visualise, chalk up your hands twice, look at the route, final thought and go. If you have anything to say to your belayer, like 'watch me at the third bolt', do it before your routine. If you get interrupted any time between starting your routine and stepping on to the rock, start again. Your routine is your trigger to help you gather your thoughts and narrow your focus to enter the flow state of mind.

Often when I ask climbers if they have a routine they say no. When I ask them what they do pre-climb they do exactly the same thing each time. They have a routine, but just don't really know it. That's kind of how it should be, but it will help you if you are aware of it to use under pressure.

A routine really needs to be natural so when you're doing it in practice you're not really thinking about it.

Your routine could be as simple as this: you squeak your boots clean, chalk your hands, picture what you want to do, have a final thought and go.

If you do a routine before every route or problem it should not take long. When the pressure is not on and you're doing your routine, at some point you will climb really well. When the pressure is on you can think back to when you used the routine and you climbed great. Go to the bank and make a withdrawal of those positive images of success. It worked then and it will work now. It's consistent.

In the beginning, your routine probably won't flow like it should; play around with it. What you're looking for is to do exactly the same thing every time, but to be unaware of it. Simple and natural is what you're looking for so when the pressure is on, you can just go into your routine click, click, click, go to the final thought and climb. You then know your actions and thoughts every step of the way. There's just no room for any negativity; you've done it so many times before.

When I practised in that caravan in France for competitions – walking out, waving to the crowd, tying into the rope and visualising the climbing – that was my rehearsal. It was consistent and took out the variables. However, it was not my routine. My on-sight routine remained the same which was: visualise, chalk up, positive final thought then start climbing.

Your final thought before you set off is also important and you have to decide what it should be. It will depend on the type of route you are doing and what your main focus should be. How aggressive is the climb? Is it a long endurance route with a boulder problem at the finish or a boulder problem start with endurance at the end?

If you are about to set out on a fifty-metre endurance route I would say your final thought does not want to be 'I need to be super aggressive.' You don't want to go out all guns blazing, overgripping and getting pumped halfway. It is all about saving energy for when you really need it. Your final thought might be more like 'smooth controlled focus'. If you're about to do a four-move sit-down start with two sharp underclings for your first move, then you're obviously going to need to be super aggressive right from the off. Your final thought in that case might be 'focused aggression'. When I was bouldering it was nearly always 'focused aggression'. For me, the word focus meant precision and accuracy. Remember, the best technique is the one executed correctly.

Find what works for you, take that final thought into your climb, keep concentrating and stay in the present.

There is one more part of a routine which is important and often overlooked. It is the end of your routine, but definitely still part of it – don't forget it.

After you've made your attempt (it might be a boulder problem or redpoint) if you are successful you reinforce it by banking it and telling yourself, 'That's like me.'

If you are unsuccessful, it's history and you must forget about it, let it go. That's the end of your routine.

Jack Nicklaus is the most successful golfer of all time, winning eighteen majors, compared to Tiger Woods who has won fifteen. He famously maintained that he had never used more than two putts per green on the last day of a major. There are four majors per year and I bet he must've been playing for twenty years – that's something like 2,000 putts which he generally thought he hadn't messed up. Of course, he missed some putts and on occasion three-putted on greens. He just couldn't remember them. He is another master of banking success and completely forgetting failure. It's the mind of a champion.

'I TELL MYSELF THE NEXT GO WILL BE THE ONE, EVERY TIME. WHEN I'M TRYING SOMETHING AND I KNOW I CAN CLIMB IT THEN EVERY TIME WHEN I START CLIMB- ING I TELL MYSELF THAT'S THE ONE GO WHEN IT WILL HAPPEN. "THIS WILL BE THE ONE." IF IT DOESN'T HAP- PEN THEN I DO EXACTLY THE SAME THING THE NEXT GO TILL IT HAPPENS.'

ALEX MEGOS

'Like I said I always pick up positive thoughts, so if I feel like today the conditions are the best then I think about the conditions. If I feel like on my warm-up I was the strongest ever I visualise my warm-up. I think that was such a good feeling and I will use that. If there is nothing positive I will probably try and think of a piece of climbing when I felt really good two weeks or a month ago. The ritual is that if it's a really hard route, I tie in and put my shoes on then I maybe wait twenty seconds, maybe two minutes. I just like to feel I'm ready. Sometimes when I have my shoes on I think it's not time yet and I'll wait one more minute. It's like the energy is in my body and something tells me this is the moment. This is the big difference between outdoors and competitions because in competition you put your shoes on and you're just waiting. You don't know whether you will be told to climb now or in five minutes, because you are waiting for the previous climber to fall off. For me this is one of the hardest parts of the competition. If the climber before slips off the second move then sometimes I think it's not my time yet. I feel I need this psychological preparation for the last three or four minutes till I feel like my mind is prepared into this psychological mode.

ADAM ONDRA

You have to catch the moment. The harder the route gets the more important it is. For bouldering I feel it's even more important; it's one hundred per cent. Everything has to be so precise. If it's a three-move problem it's so important, even grabbing the first holds. You can't lose even one per cent of energy in bouldering.'

Feel when you're READY → THIS IS YOUR Moment!

Adam Ondra
in Flatanger
Cave, Norway

© Claudia Ziegler

'I'm already tied in, I've got my shoes on then I'm building the energy and focusing, to think about the route and try and build the energy in. It's really about the process of clearing your mind and preparing yourself for the ascent, bringing the energy into your core and psyching yourself up.

You need to create space where you're not thinking and that's the balance when climbing: not thinking too much but trying super super hard. For sure breathing helps me, taking deep breaths, almost with those breaths pushing out the distractions. One of those big distractions, as I said, is your mind, so get focused and serious but at the same time you have to kind of think, "Whatever, let's go climbing." To be able to do the climb you have to take it super seriously and have to want it more than anything but at the same time you can't take yourself too seriously because that's going to work against you. You have to want it more than anything but at the same time not really give a hoot.'

CHRIS SHARMA

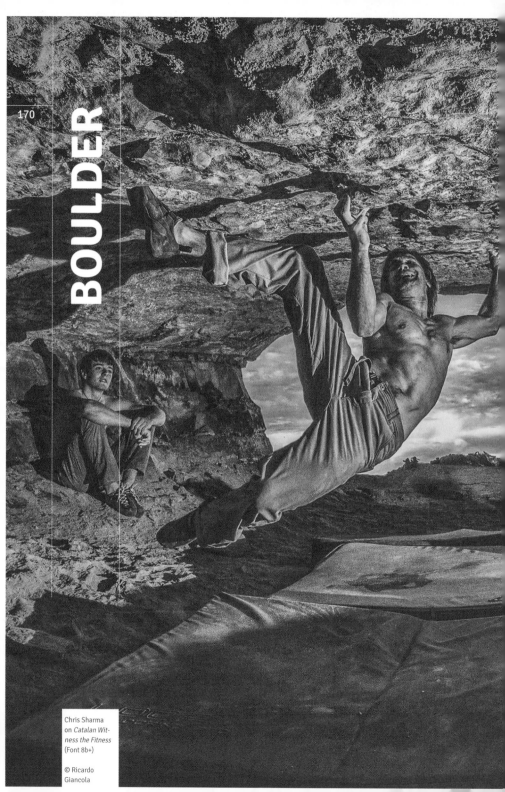

BOULDER

Chris Sharma
on *Catalan Witness the Fitness*
(Font 8b+)

© Ricardo
Giancola

Bouldering is now a well-established and respected form of climbing.

It is practically a sport in its own right, as there are many people who only boulder and never do routes or any other form of climbing. It's a very social form of climbing, as you are with your partners all the time and able to talk. You can work on problems figuring out the moves at the same time as opposed to watching someone climb high up on a face while you belay.

JOHN GILL

'SOPHISTICATED ROCK TECHNIQUE IS NOT A PART OF OUR PRIMAL HERITAGE.'

Bouldering is the most powerful and explosive form of climbing and therefore can at times require an aggressive mindset because everything happens so quickly. It requires a lot of precision along with delicacy in your climbing. It might take many days and hundreds of falls before you send a hard problem. I like to think of it this way: you only fail in bouldering if you stop trying. In the attempt, it's just experience. When picturing what you want to achieve everything must be very precise. On difficult problems, you don't have any time to adjust feet or fingers. In your visualisation, I would combine kinaesthetic with internal perspective imagery. What you want to do is try to create a picture of precision in the moves and how they are going to flow. When you are attempting a problem, just trying to do the individual moves, imagine piecing them together, visualise the link, what it will feel like to stick to moves from the ground. Try to feel the exhilaration you will have when you piece all the moves together and complete the problem. Start to compose yourself for the fight, go through your routine and climb.

'I boulder my best when I'm just out with my friends having fun. I try to block everything out, don't over-think. I try to turn my brain off and just climb in the moment. It's the art of letting go; I'm just psyched. Where I'm really motivated on something I visualise it a lot. All day every day, like an obsession. Before they go to bed some people count sheep; I'm just thinking about my project and visualising. I use it more when I'm going to bed; going to sleep you can kind of decompress from the day. Just think about what's most important to you and that's rock climb-ing. When you look up at a project you can feel re-ally super nervous. I like to think about what makes me happy, makes me excited in life. It can be things not even related to climbing. Just to give you some clearance in your head and put you in an uplifted place. Just enjoy it, look where you are and what you're doing, enjoying the here. Whether it's a pass or fail I'm going to try really hard and it's going to be amazing. I try to be as positive as possible. The only thing I know going into the day is I'm going to try really hard. That's the only guarantee I can put on my climbing.'

JIMMY WEBB

Marc Le Menestrel was at the very forefront of redpointing in the 1980s doing the hardest routes in the world at the time. In the 1990s doing boulder problems like *L'Alchimiste* (Font 8b) he pushed boul-dering standards. Living in Fontainebleau he was very powerful and stylish to watch.

This is what Marc says about bouldering:

'Your great mistake is to climb as if you were the climber you think you are. You are never who you think you are. You are always much more than this. And even more when you are climbing. Beyond what you think you are, you are also your body that feels without thinking, your belayer below who encourages you, your friends around and even all the climbers who inspired you across the world and for generations. Extending your consciousness to whatever you dare to include, you may think that when you are climbing, you are even the rock itself. In this sense, you are also the holds and the grains of sandstone or limestone or granite that enter your fingers and your soles. So when you are climbing, you can think that you are the rock and that you hold your body to make it climb. Then, to master your mind when you are climbing is to let the rock move your body up and ask your mind to just let this happen. Be the rock!'

MARC
LE MENESTREL

ALEX MEGOS

'HARD BOULDERING REQUIRES PATIENCE AND LOTS AND LOTS OF TRIES.'

'For bouldering I feel it's even more important, it's one hundred per cent. Everything has to be so precise. If it's a three-move problem it's so important, even grabbing the first holds. You can't lose even one per cent of energy in bouldering.'

ADAM ONDRA

Hannes Huch
on *Le Parfum
des Couleurs*
(Font 7c)

© Marion Hett

ON-SIGHT

An on-sight is walking up to the bottom of a route with no prior knowledge and climbing it bottom to top with no falls.

You have just one go; any weight on the rope is a failure. Knowing this, there is obviously quite a lot of pressure. Is it more pressure than redpoint, bouldering, trad or competitions? My view: it really depends how much you want it. They are all equal in my eyes because if you really want it there's going to be an immense amount of pressure.

With soloing it involves death or serious injury and that pressure is different. I have done on-sights which I have specifically trained for as they had been goals for a long time. They are the ones I remember because the pressure was really on. I would wait for perfect conditions, be well rested, with good skin, and for that reason I had the best chance of success when the crunch time came. I can clearly remember standing at the bottom of some of them looking up thinking, 'This is it.' The training is done, the test is just about to start.

On-sight is a little bit like a game of fantasy. You have to use your imagination. Before your attempt, you should be visualising how you think the route will feel. I would use kinaesthetic and internal visualisation combined. You want to picture your hands feeling the holds, see your foot placements and feel your body fighting its way up the route. Picture the struggle and be ready for all eventualities.

Don't hold back. You have to take risks because you don't know if the moves are going to work until you go into them. Embrace the anxiety, go for it. Absolute commitment is what's needed. It is just that little bit harder on-sight because you're committing to moves you don't know will work.

The key is convincing yourself beforehand that all the moves you're committing to will work.

It may be that you do your hardest on-sights on climbs you weren't trying to on-sight. That was my experience when I did *Heisse Finger* (IX, F7c) and *Pol Pot* (F7c+) which were the first on-sights of those grades. They were great, but I remember more the ones that I trained specifically for like *Equinox* (5.12c), also probably the first route of that grade to be on-sighted. I was so revved up at the bottom of that route and just wanted it so bad.

Get your mind prepared early and be ready to feel nervous. Those nerves and anxiety will help you focus and give you strength.

Visualise and imagine exactly what you have to do when the big day comes. Use the techniques you have learnt, inhibit the negatives and focus on the goal.

'I try to put as little pressure on myself as possible. So I try to tell myself that it's not important if I on-sight the route or not. If the result doesn't matter, I tend to climb much more relaxed and free, which means that I climb more efficiently. I climb with more risk in terms of doing insecure moves, which is necessary to on-sight at your limit. I think the preparation consists of making yourself believe that the result is not as important as the process itself. The more freely you climb in your mind, the better you will climb.'

ALEX MEGOS

WISDOM

'In on-sighting it's totally multitasking. If you have to really think how you want to take this crimp – Like this? Which foothold shall I use? – you will be too slow, the flow of climbing will not be there. It's better in that situation to let your instincts take the decision for you. On-sighting is about taking risks. The risk of not hesitating. I don't hesitate. Almost never while on-sighting. I just get into a position and have a clear beta in my mind from the ground. I keep climbing and if it looks different I'll decide in the flick of a switch to change beta. I will do that, but importantly I will be super confident that the decision is right and that's why I go for it. I don't doubt my decision, I just go for it. If I had to really consider in my mind whether this is a good decision or not I would hesitate and lose two or three seconds, and that's just too much. I'm sometimes super nervous before I climb. The perfect situation is when I pull my feet off the ground, the nerves go and I'm in the zone. It doesn't always happen. The more pressure I have, the harder it is. Sometimes it's just not working out. Very rarely if I start climbing badly does it turn out for the better. In that situation, I just climb badly, that's it.'

ADAM ONDRA

WISDOM

REDPOINT

Redpointing is where the highest level of difficulty is achieved while climbing routes.

The very hardest routes, like *La Dura Dura* (F9b+) at Oliana in Spain or *Silence* (F9c) in the Flatanger Cave in Norway, take the best climbers in the world today years to climb. Repeated visits are required with specific training plans put in place. On each failure, there is a realisation that more power is needed or perhaps more endurance or better conditions.

After continual practice on moves for long periods the time eventually comes and reality dawns that you should now be finishing the route. That is when pressure is at its highest. It is the last thing you think about before bed and your waking thought. It can be all encompassing and take over your life. You will have probably fallen many times all over the route and perhaps even not been able to do one of the moves for a while.

These thoughts of falling must be put out of your mind and replaced by the memories of when you have done the moves when you were at your best – when you were strong, had good skin and conditions were perfect.

Reading your climbing diary will help bring back those memories.

When you work the route and are linking sections, try to get the feeling of what it's going to feel like climbing it from the ground. At some point, start to picture ending the route.

While redpointing and you do a good link or maybe do the crux move for the first time, reinforce it and tell yourself, 'That's like me.' Be cocky and tell yourself, 'That was a great link, I'm going to do it.' Bank your success and write it in your diary. Similarly, if you are not doing great one day don't get frustrated. Forget it, blame it on the conditions or your skin. Remembering a bad day's climbing will never do you any good.

'If I'm attempting a really hard redpoint then I will use visualisation. Actually, people might think that on-sighting is more stressful, but I think it is a total contradiction. On a redpoint or long-term project you've got certain things that you are afraid of, like a certain move that you fell off twenty times or a foothold that is slippery. Let's say there are just so many nightmare places that can occupy your mind. Whereas in on-sighting you don't know the route, you don't know the nightmare places, you just go. That's why I've always found redpointing so much harder. With redpointing, I think in the beginning you can be too focused on the hardest move and then you completely mess up the easy beginning. You might not fall, but you mess it up and you get to the crux just way too tired. That is a very common mistake. Some people have their project and focus on the crux sections, but they completely neglect making the easy sections really easy. Even if it's a 9a and the first ten metres are 7a, it's still pretty important how you climb the 7a, even though 7a and 9a is a completely different world. We are talking about only one or two per cent, but that can be the difference between falling off and sticking the next move. The percentages are just tiny. If you start climbing on the bottom perfectly, it's rare that you climb badly at the end. On redpoints, you know what's coming. When you know the route perfectly, you can switch on autopilot and keep going – no fear, no doubt just keep going. In that the situation, I think you can climb closer to your limit.'

ADAM ONDRA

WISDOM

'When you start a project and it's super fun, then once you realise you can do it the anxiety sets in and the mental struggle starts. Interestingly, since I've become a dad there has been so much less worry and it's been easier to tap into the positive mindset. I have less time to climb, but it's much better quality. I was in Oliana not so long ago and I saw people stressing out on their projects. In this moment of my life, it seems a more superficial thing to worry about. When you are dealing with your child there's so much more real-life stress. When I get to go climbing nowadays I'm just so much more psyched, it's a good day and I'm not too worried, and because of that you climb better. It's not easy keeping the concentration on long routes. For every success there's a thousand failures. That's what I mean by just keep trying and trying until you just go climbing. One's desire to achieve a route is certainly the most interesting moment on a climb. When you are super pumped going through a crux and then maybe you get to a place, not really a rest, but just a shakeout, you're just super accelerated and could be just about to fall off. How do you calm yourself down and relax? You've got to breathe into it and slow your heart down. I imagine breathing space into my muscles and visualise breathing out the lactic acid. I'm breathing in fresh energy. How do you stay focused? That's just what we live to do, that's the task in hand. There are little tools you can use, but you just need to be super psyched to achieve that goal. You have to want it a lot, and to be able

CHRIS SHARMA

to do that you have to keep yourself together. When you're panicking you just have to calm yourself down. You've got to try and auto-trick yourself into not having expectations.'

Just keep trying and trying!

'When redpointing a hard route I tell myself that it doesn't matter if I get up or not. I'll always be able to give it another try if this one fails so I've got as much time as I want and no pressure. That makes me climb more freely and relaxed and in general better. When I'm resting between attempts I think the next try will be the one, for sure! Even if it won't be the next one, it'll be the one after that one, for sure! But no matter how many tries it'll take, I'll do it!'

ALEX MEGOS

W1500M

Margo Hayes, born 1998 in the USA, is a hugely talented climber. She says, 'As in many sports, mental strength is just as important, if not more so, than physical ability.'

Aged eighteen, she climbed *Bad Girls Club*, her first F9a. In 2016, she became Junior World Champion both in lead and bouldering. In 2017, Margo did *La Rambla* in Spain which made her the first woman to climb F9a+.

MARGO HAYES

'AS IN MANY SPORTS, MENTAL STRENGTH IS JUST AS IMPORTANT, IF NOT MORE SO, THAN PHYSICAL ABILITY.'

'I do a lot of visualisation. For instance, if I have a route or competition I can visualise that. I do it in my head so many times it becomes an obsession and that's part of who I am. It helps me because when I'm on the climb it feels like I have done it before. I think you need to write down goals so you can really see it, read it and focus on it. You can then become more comfortable with believing it and think that it's possible. I write my goals down for the day or the week and then I have future goals. I have a planner and I will write a lot in that. I also use sticky notes to remind me of my goals. Sometimes the goals are just for me to stay grounded and believe in myself. It's like an affirmation. I keep it to myself to come back to as I don't always feel great mentally. When I'm mentally down it helps me to get right back up there again. If you can learn how to get back up from that low point then you can come back stronger.

I was a gymnast and since I was really small, about seven or eight, I used to write down goals. My parents thought I was crazy. It's just something I've always done. In order to really achieve a goal it needs to be specific because if you just say I wanna get stronger you don't really have any way of measuring it. Whereas, if you say I want to do that climb or do well in that competition you really have a way to track that. When you have a goal it's like the golden carrot up there. If it is not clear, it's harder to have the motivation.

I think more often than not people don't succeed because of mental blocks. If you want to push yourself and reach your full potential you have to focus on what's going on mentally. Often I feel when I'm climbing my best, I can't think about what I'm thinking about, if that makes any sense. I feel so in the moment I'm not thinking about the past or the future. There are times when I talk to myself on routes or when I'm resting trying to keep myself positive. It's important to be present and stay in the moment. Let go of things which don't matter and concentrate on things which are right in front of you, whether it's a boulder problem or competition. If you create your own glass ceiling it's going to be harder to break through. I think it's something that comes naturally to everyone to create: "This is my kind of level." For myself, I think it's important to press that ceiling up, to just break it and remove it altogether. Knowing this, no route is too hard or move too difficult.

MARGO HAYES

I think a lot of it comes down to a decision; what you wanna focus on. Sometimes it's easier to fail, but to push through that mental struggle and then succeed in the end, that's what's truly rewarding. For me, I climb my best when I'm happy and smiling, when I feel grounded.'

SOLOING

Climbing without ropes is obviously extremely serious. It should never be tackled unless you really know what you are doing and even then it carries great risk.

I can still remember my first solo and being totally shocked at how much harder it was to climb with no ropes. I was only doing an easy climb that I had done before. I really scared myself and did not do it again for another year. In the early 1980s, I did a lot of soloing. It was one of my main objectives, to solo grades and climbs which had previously been unimaginable.

I had a circuit on my local limestone crag, Stoney Middleton, which I did every day. I had to get used to being in the situation where any mistake would be serious. I would wake up thinking about the routes I wanted to do while on my circuit. To avoid pressure, I would keep the routes I wanted to do to myself. If it doesn't feel right when soloing you must always give yourself the option of reversing down and walking away if possible.

For training, in the winter of 1982, we would do a lot of top-roping doing the same climb repeatedly just to get really pumped. It was long before indoor climbing and no one had a car. Rather than hitch a lift we would just walk to the nearest crag from the cafe which was in Stoney Middleton. One of my favourite routes to work out on was called *Scarab*. It is now graded E6 6b (around F7b or 7b+). It is about twelve metres long, bouldery at the start with the crux move at the top, which is a rockover with a long lock-off and reach to a good horizontal break. Back then, it was one of the hardest routes around.

I was relatively inexperienced in soloing. I could top-rope it quite a few times without falling and I knew the route very well. One day I said to my mate Neil Molnar (Neil sadly died in 1983 soloing in Wales), 'I'm gonna solo it now. I'm going to get some more chalk from my tent.' When I came back a couple of minutes later my head was in a completely different space. I had come out of the zone and I was very nervous. All I could think about was, 'I have to solo it now.' I was unprepared for the pressure and fear.

I barely made it up the start then shook my way across the traverse completely overgripping every hold. For some reason it never occurred to me to try and climb down or jump from the start of the traverse, which is possible. I just carried on because I said, 'I'm going to do it this go.' You have got far too much to lose doing something like that just because you said you were going to. I can still remember reaching for the break on the final crux move, watching my hand in slow motion getting the good hold, and the relief.

My thoughts looking back now are: 'What a complete idiot.' It was much harder than anything anyone had soloed in England before.

Soloing is about total control of your climbing, otherwise you simply won't survive.

I never put that pressure on myself again while soloing. I would just tell myself, 'I'm going up for a look.' I didn't like people being around and didn't get photos on any of my hard solos. It just felt like more pressure and I didn't like the thought of someone seeing me fall or that it could be the last photo!

Soloing is not about taking risks. It's about smooth, controlled, focused climbing with your mind absolutely in the present.

Alex Honnold is absolutely and without doubt at the forefront of soloing. He is a well-rounded climber. At the time of writing, he holds the record for the fastest ascent of *The Nose* on El Cap in one hour, fifty-eight minutes and seven seconds (with Tommy Caldwell). He soloed Half Dome, along with routes like *The Phoenix* (5.13a). He did the complete traverse of the Fitz Roy Massif in Patagonia with Tommy Caldwell. His biggest accomplishment is certainly the first ever solo of El Capitan via *Freerider* (5.12d) which he did in spring 2017. *Freerider* is 914 metres, thirty-five pitches, normally taking four days to climb. Alex's solo ascent took three hours and fifty-six minutes.

Outrageously impressive.

I asked Alex how he prepared mentally for a big solo. Here's what he said:

'This is obviously a big question since it encompass-es a lot of different aspects of climbing. At the min-imum, I need to know the moves and memorise the actual sequences. Beyond that, there's a certain amount of self-confidence and self-belief that are required to get off the ground.

Then above all that is the visualisation and prepa-ration that ensure that the climb actually goes smoothly, hopefully. So basically, to prepare for a hard solo I try to climb it beforehand, memorise the moves and then replay the movement mentally with an emphasis on how it will feel ropeless.

It's important for me to think about how secure or insecure the moves will feel and the actual sensa-tion of my fingers and toes touching the rock. I want to make sure there are no surprises when I'm on the wall, since anything unforeseen has the potential to rattle me or affect my performance.

So the more I can visualise beforehand the less likely anything surprising will happen. Ideally, when I'm doing a hard solo I'm not really think-ing about anything. My mind should be clear and I should be just executing the moves. The reality is that my mind sometimes drifts a bit, especially on easy climbing, and any random thoughts might drift through like what to eat later or appreciating the view. For very hard solos, my mind should be blank and I should just be physically moving. The

whole point of visualising beforehand and memorising all the moves is so that the rational part of
my brain doesn't need to be engaged during a solo.
I don't need to be wondering things like, "Does my
left foot go up first or should I reach for the right
hand now?" I should already know exactly what to
do, which minimises the need for thinking. Before
I pull on, it is a little more varied. I'm often a little
nervous, since no matter how prepared I am I'm still
setting out to do something that I've never done
before or has maybe never been done full stop. So
there's always a little uncertainty.

In general, I try to just put myself on autopilot
and do whatever it is I'm setting out to do. I think
that maybe the key part of visualisation for me is to
imagine any possible scenario so that I'm not surprised during a big solo. I visualise cruising through
the crux, but I also think about what it will be like
if I am more tired than expected and my fingers feel
greasy.

That way, when the moment arrives, one way or
another, I'll know exactly what to do and won't hesitate at all. The thing about soloing is that you can't
exactly practise it over and over since the consequences are high. Visualisation fills in the gaps. It
allows you to "practise" as much as you need with
no consequences.'

ALEX HONNOLD

Mich Kemeter
soloing in the
Verdon Gorge

© Alex Buisse

Mich Kemeter is at the forefront of extreme slacklining and holds numerous world records. He slacklined the Lost Arrow Spire in Yosemite on-sight solo which is terrifying to watch online. He also solo-BASE climbs, doing some hard stuff in the Verdon. Solo-BASE climbing is without ropes, but with a small parachute which may or may not save you.

Mich's views on solo-BASE climbing :

'"Do it or don't do it. There's no trying!"
Your body will only carry you as far as you are mentally able to go. By that I mean, you don't literally have to go anywhere to be somewhere, you are already there. That's my starting point, the one from which I take on "new ways". Where no soul has gone before. To change the borders of my thinking, to stay alive is the motivation which burns inside of me.

"I always have a plan: from A to F. F stands for Fxxx!"
If I face complex climbing without a rope in combination with difficult climbing, if all I have is a BASE unit on my back then the imagination mentioned above is the trigger. It is the spark that ignites the fire and the reason why I started skydiving in the first place. The realisation took years to provide the security standard needed. This process totally changed my attitude towards life because you have to learn to let go in these special and extreme moments. I had to learn to simply be.

Change is my only constant to keep this creativity going and is necessary to feed my determination. The joy as well as the composure of being "in the present" reflects itself for me in the quality of everything and constantly lights up my horizon. "Choose life. Choose future."

Principles, rituals and memories are only parts of shards that diffract the light and reflect it. Without them it would be impossible for me to learn. For me it's important that everything should be made as simple as possible, but not simpler. That's why it was very important for me to learn step by step. "If you are not able to do something special at the moment, it's not that you can't ever do it." At the beginning of my solo-BASE experience this motto was a very important teacher for me as far as patience and acceptance go.

These principles and experiences which I often encounter on the fringes of my limits are close to everyday life and converge on the same level: well-being. Especially when I exercise hard sequences it is important that I feel good doing it or if I do something that I can't cope with. An inattentiveness in these moments can decide the future. To have the absolute control over something that you can feel and experience only once is a moment of absolute concentration. This can be described with the so-called state of flow. Even when the situation was exhausting and filled with fear I could learn from it. Fear has become a constant companion and even a good friend.

For me it is important to listen to yourself and learn. To learn to feel if it is worth the consequences that you can cause. I like to ponder things and put them on the imaginary scale; unforeseen things happen fast and often with a reason. Preparation is very important. The whole range of questions have to be answered beforehand so every moment of the actual doing is executed with a clear mind and in a precise manner.

I have experienced such control of thought and emotion to absolute perfection in my previous careers as a pistol-shooter and a "free solo high liner". That's why the first time of letting go in the realm of solo-BASE climbing was a familiar situation, although I had only previously experienced it mentally. This feeling where you leave the secure grip and move forward into this "new" world where no gravity exists. The total commitment of flying comes after about three seconds when the body position itself determines whether you collide with the wall or fly free.

The greatest difference between solo-BASE climbing and traditional free-solo climbing is the mental component: in case something goes fatally wrong. If a hold breaks there is still a narrow chance to cheat the hangman. But for me this feeling is treacherous because it lessens my attention for the moment; the weight of three kilos [the parachute] should not be underestimated when you climb hard.'

MICH KEMETER

— ■ —

COMPETITION

Kilian Fischhuber
at the World
Championships
in Paris, 2012

© Elias Holz-
knecht

Competition climbing is not like normal climbing, which is competing with yourself. In competition climbing, it's about beating other people.

For that reason, mentally the challenge is very different. Yes it's you against the climb, and fundamentally that's all it should be. You working out the next move in front of you. In your head, however, there are more distractions. You only have one attempt and you don't decide when that is, can't wait for conditions. You might like climbing in the evening and you're competing in the morning. You might be anxious to beat a certain competitor. Maybe you don't like the look of the route. Perhaps you climbed poorly in the previous competition and want to make amends. There are so many different factors that can play on your mind.

For this reason you need to start thinking early on about all these different types of challenges and distractions. If they are not going to help with your climbing they need to be rationalised and inhibited from your thoughts.

Your goal is to climb with a flow state of mind, fully focused on the exam paper put in front of you.

Whether you like the look of the climb or not that's your test of the day. It's a competition and you have to get on with it. Not only that, you have to make yourself enjoy the challenge.

Every route or boulder problem you face before you pull on you've got to think, 'I like the look of this one.'

What better way then than to use external perspective visualisation. Sit there in the crowd and watch yourself climb with your competitors sat next to you. It could just make you that bit more competitive, making you focus more and giving you the edge. I would definitely then use kinaesthetic and internal visualisation imagery to imagine what you're about to climb.

At the end of the day it's you against what you're about to climb. You have to do the move presented in front of you, the next one after that and, hopefully, if you're strong enough you will end up on top.

One of the important factors in competitions is inhibiting all the negatives and to narrow your field of focus down as small and as tight as can be. It's possible then to enter the flow state of mind. What Adam, Killian and Anna have to say in the following pages regarding competitions is so strong. Between them they have won over 20 overall world cup and world championship titles!

'Before a competition, I visualise because it's an on-sight.

I visualise it three or four times as perfectly as possible, moving my feet and my hands, making it real. I even try to imagine which muscles I'm going to use. Just before I start climbing I don't visualise the route itself. I visualise a certain moment in the recent time like one week before when I felt like I was climbing perfectly, when I felt strong and I had the perfect flow. In my mind, if I felt so good one week ago why should it be different today because I'm even better, I'm rested and better trained? I slept perfectly and I've been super cautious about everything, so it just has to be better today. This is the way I boost my self-confidence.

One thing about risk: when I'm in a situation when I know the next move is insecure, for me, from my experience, yes I do take a risk and fall too early sometimes. In the end, in the case of competitions, I go there to take the victory. If I'm fourth or eighth I don't really give a toss. I know that if I hesitate on the route even for a few seconds my margin is definitely that I will not be able to win. My way is just going for it all out. In this way, I know I have a good chance to win. If it's insecure and I don't really know if the next hold is good then I trust my intuition. If I have to jump for it, I just hope the next hold is good rationally for me in the most probable way to get to the victory. Staying on the safe side it is probable that you let the victory go without actually trying. If I get stuck, I might get to the next section, but I will probably get tired and fall in the next few moves. Rationality is good before climbing, but intuition is best while climbing.'

ADAM ONDRA

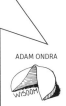

'I listen to loud music in the five-minute break between boulders. It helps me to really focus on positive memories from the past. Sometimes I think about boulders I have completed or different positive things to help me concentrate. I try to be in the moment and enjoy what I'm doing and not to think about the competition too much. In the end I think about climbing and reduce it to what's important. It's not that you win in the end. What do you want to do? You want to complete the boulder. That's why you're on the mat, it's why you're there. To only think about the climb is what helps.

For me, to climb my best I definitely have to care about it; the not-giving-a-damn approach does not work for me. If I want to complete something I have to really want it somehow. Sometimes in competitions, because every attempt counts and because you've given one attempt away, you might be more focused on the next attempt. I am a little bit aggressive then or upset for giving an attempt away, because I know I can do it and I want to prove it to myself.

I think the tricky part is in those four or five minutes between problems, depending what round you are in. If you flash your boulder, it's easy because you don't have time to think. If you fall, that's when it gets tricky. I step back and look at the boulder again, trying to see my mistakes, and again just try and focus on the boulder. What's important to me is how to get to the top. In bouldering, the thinking happens on the mat.

I also try to blend out the other problems I've done or might not have done. If I think about the fall I've just had then I'm negative, so I just try and think in the moment again where I am now. When you hear in the speaker that someone else has topped out it's easy for it to disturb your concentration. I've caught myself doing maths in the break, thinking, "She just did that, what place can I be in?" That's actually a very bad

ANNA STÖHR

thing to do for me. In fact, it is bad for anyone who does that! It is good to know what you have to do because it makes you very concentrated. The best tip is listen to yourself, to not try and imitate someone else, but listen to what's best for you.'

'When it comes to early preparation for a competition I always try to visualise things. When I was younger, I used to visualise the moves and arriving at the top. Later, I tried to visualise more the things that would disturb me if I wasn't prepared. I thought about pressures, for instance a lot of people and journalists asking me the same questions like "You want to win, this is your comp." Or just the pressure of having to perform in front of the crowd. These are the things I thought through, nothing in great detail, but a little bit so when I came there it wasn't like, "Oh my God, there's so many people." I was prepared for a certain level, not for every move or doing jumps.

When it comes to mental preparation, like just before the comp or the movement, you're really nervous. Minutes before I went out I always tried to put it into perspective. What's my goal, why am I doing this, what if I don't perform well, what if I win? Then I tried to get a bit of distance from this so it's not quite as important without losing the punch. There's a thin line between going there and not caring, and going there and not being too overwhelmed with what I had to do. The last stage when I was under the boulder and I was about to do it I took one deep breath and thought, "Let's go for it." It can happen or it can't happen, but I can only try. This reduced a little bit of the pressure, I think. When you boulder it is so short it's really hard to get into the flow moment, so I tried to get into a fake flow before I started climbing, like you have pulled on to it. I just go into a feeling of "Just climb, it's just climbing. It's not success or failure. Just do what you do." In bouldering

KILIAN
FISCHHUBER

competition, it's hard because you know what you have to do, you know how many tries you have left. As soon as you touch the first hold, thinking is almost impossible. If you do, you're on the mat again. I think in lead climbing the mental aspect is harder because you have time to think. If you have time to think, you have time to make mistakes in your head. In bouldering, you think and it's almost over.

What we often forget about success or people who win a lot, regarding mental things, is why they are so strong. I think that success makes you successful. If you do well once, like you did the first boulder, you will do the second boulder and the third and it gets momentum. It's the same thing the other way round. We should look at people that have bad times and then come back. I always say, if you win once it is easy to win the second time. To keep focus between problems, I always tried to have a nice time, talked to the other competitors. Then two minutes before I had to climb I stopped talking and tried to focus on myself again. If you are so self-obsessed and focused to blank out everything I think a lot gets lost. If you do all the four problems first try it's pretty certain that you're going to win. It's more about yourself, if you're having a good time, if you're relaxed. Two minutes before you start, you focus again. There must be a place for having fun and being relaxed otherwise this whole thing is just work. It's not work, it's climbing, it's a cool sport so why not enjoy it!'

Anna Stöhr
doing what
she does best:
winning!

© Elias Holz-
knecht

TRAD

Pete Whittaker
climbing on grit

© Michael
Hutton

When I started climbing in the late 1970s what is now called traditional or 'trad' climbing was the only type of climbing there was. In the UK at least there was no redpoint, on-sight; no real quality climbing walls or competitions. People did boulder, particularly on gritstone, but it wasn't really thought of as climbing and certainly got no publicity in the climbing magazines; needless to say this was decades before the internet!

Back then you never saw bolts and only rarely saw pitons. When you saw the latter they were generally relics from old artificial climbs. All your protection or gear had to be placed from the ground up. It's a fantastic, pure form of climbing, as you can imagine the route being just the same as when the first ascensionist walked up to the bottom of it. Traditional climbing differs markedly from sport or bolt-protected climbing for a few reasons. First you have to look at the route and be certain what type of equipment you're going to take for the pitch. You don't want to take everything you own, as you will be just too weighed down with gear.

Normally you will have no prior knowledge of where the hard or easy climbing is, where to rest, etc. This is the tricky bit and is very similar to having the mindset of doing an on-sight.

In fact it's virtually the same except you are more conscious of how far you are going to fall and whether your last piece of protection is good or not. It can be very exciting and I loved the years placing gear, doing run-outs and scaring myself. I got lazy as I got older, and once I started clipping bolts in the late 1980s I seldom did trad routes again except on gritstone where bolts and pitons are forbidden.

I think because traditional climbing is generally on-sight when I started doing on-sights and competitions I adapted well. When you are trad climbing you are always fighting, trying to get as high as you possibly can to get more gear in higher up the route, even if you have already fallen off low down. Because you don't know what kind of climbing you are going to face or what kind of gear you're going to be getting you have to study the route carefully and make decisions from previous experiences.

Keeping yourself safe is the first task of trad climbing. You may get some idea of how serious a route is or how scary from the description in the guidebook. Get your gear sorted and arranged with a view to how you think you will use it. It helps to place your runners in exactly the same place on your harness so you know where they will be. Because trad climbing can be dangerous you need to be prepared for the fact you might get scared.

Remember that the fear and anxiety you will feel as you climb will not be a bad thing as long as it's controlled.

It's going get you focused; it needs addressing though and it's a good idea to visualise how you are going to feel emotionally. If anything goes wrong, which it probably will at some point if you climb a lot, you need to know how you will react and be ready.

Next you want to look for places where you might be able to get a rest and then finally where the difficult climbing might be. Visualise the whole thing in precise detail using the techniques we have previously gone through in the visualisation chapter. Go through your pre-climb routine and off you go. Stay in the present and enjoy the climb, or, which often happened to me, if you're climbing on the sea cliffs at Gogarth in North Wales get ready for an epic! Still fun though.

I asked a couple of climbers, Pete Whittaker and Mayan Smith-Gobat, who are without doubt right at the very top of the game with regards to trad climbing, for their thoughts. Pete is primarily a trad climber, but has also done some amazing first ascents, particularly horrendous-looking off-width cracks in the States. An off-width crack would be normally wider than a fist, but not big enough to get your whole body inside. It's a difficult size and hard to master; it's physically awkward and uncomfortable. In that field, he's probably the best in the world at the moment.

Here is what Pete has to say regarding trad:

'The main thing I do to prepare before a route is use visualisation. Visualisation for me isn't just taking a minute before setting off to remember the sequence and clipping position on the route; sometimes on hard and dangerous routes it can actually be a longer process than the physical part of the climbing.

It might sound strange, but I often start any visualisation with failure: what it would be like to fail, the consequences and what this would feel like.

After I've gone through all the types of failure and consequences I start to visualise myself overcome these failures one by one, until eventually I'm cruising the route. By starting from failure and getting to success, I will have covered everything, so nothing should be a surprise when I'm climbing and I should be able to deal with anything unexpected.

Also by starting at failure and getting to success it makes me feel good/strong/positive about my climbing. If I start at success and get to success, success just becomes normal, which means I'd never be able to deal with struggle or anything unexpected.

There are two types of visualisation that I use:

Type 1 [kinaesthetic imagery]: Visualise as if I am the climber on redpoint. I go through the moves – hand placement, foot placement, gear placement, how to hold each hold, pivot on each foot, every minor detail – as if I was there doing the route. It is important for me to also visualise everything under different circumstances. So for example what if I caught the crux hold wrong and couldn't readjust? What if I was too pumped to place the key bit of kit? What if I forgot to chalk up at the crucial chalking-up spot and my hands got greasy? Each and every little detail like this I imagine beforehand. I imagine how I would feel in all these other unexpected situations and then imagine myself overcoming them to eventually cruise the route. By doing this, I've covered everything in my mind worst to best (with the best being my final visual outcome) so whatever happens, I'm not surprised by it.

Type 2 [external perspective imagery]: Visualise as if you are watching yourself climb the route as an onlooker. I use this type of visualisation to help look at myself climbing. I do pretty much the same process as above and watch myself failing, then watch myself overcome all the possible outcomes that could happen on the route, until I eventually watch myself cruise the route effortlessly.

By using these two types of visualising, you can feel yourself being strong on the route (type 1), but also cement that fact in your mind by seeing yourself looking strong on the route (type 2).

The important end factor using visualisation is always success, however you have overcome all outcomes to get there.

I use these redpoint techniques on both dangerous routes and safe routes (solos, sport climbs and everything in-between), it's just there are different ways of looking at it for both.

Failure for a dangerous trad climb could mean serious injury or death, whereas failure slipping off the 5+ section of a 9a sport route after the crux would just mean severe frustration. It's just about visualising the correct possibilities and potential outcomes for each event before setting off.

It is also important for me that mental preparation and physical preparation go side by side. There is no point being able to cruise the route in your mind when you physically can't. There is no point in being able to physically cruise the route but you can't bring yourself to set off, deal with the unexpected or be a shaking bag of nerves when you do finally set off.

With on-sight trad there is less visualising moves, as I don't know what the moves are! I look as much as possible from the ground where the hard parts are and where potential gear will go. I do try and visualise what hard sections of the route will feel like (compared to other similar routes I've climbed). I try and organise gear on my harness as best as possible; make it easy to get to pieces quickly that I think might fit in important places. I generally try and have an escape or backup plan before setting off.

With on-sighting you only truly know what it is going to be like and how you will feel when you have started climbing. Within the first few metres you will generally have a good idea of how you are feeling on the route; I monitor most things from here on in.

When I'm climbing at my best, for on-sight trad climbing, my focus is on long or dangerous run-outs; when on-sight climbing I'm both focusing on the climbing and the run-out. I'm constantly judging both factors. I'm taking into account the length of run-out, the fall potential, the danger of the fall, the difficulty of climbing I've just done (in case of reversing), the climbing up ahead and the fatigue of my body. I'm constantly assessing and linking all the factors together through every move and at the end of the moves. By assessing and linking these factors together while climbing I can try and predict the best and safest option. It sounds like there are lots of things going on here, but after a while you are able to monitor all the factors in a split second and make a judgement.

Redpoint climbing – I pretty much have a different approach. I'm not assessing the situation. I know what the situation is. The important factor for me on a dangerous redpoint is to not let your adrenaline levels get too high. When you get the adrenaline levels correct, it should make you really strong on moves that you thought were difficult on top rope, but without having the leg-shake. So I'm trying to manage adrenaline levels (to get that perfect level where you feel really strong/never pumped/everything easier than it ever has been) rather than assessing the situation.'

PETE WHITTAKER

Mayan is also one of the most established trad climbers in the world today, certainly pushing standards of female rock climbing and just hard core climbing in general. She's done *Salathé Wall* on El Cap, Yosemite in a push; got the female speed record on El Cap: three hours, twenty-nine minutes (with Sean Leary). She also has the female record linking Half Dome and *The Nose*: twenty hours, fourteen minutes. Mayan also did the fifth ascent of *Riders on the Storm* on Torres Del Paine in Patagonia freeing all the pitches. It's fair to say she is an amazing, well-rounded climber.

Here is what Mayan has to say regarding trad:

'I try to consider all of the factors, analyse the level of risk and where the dangerous sections are. I like to rule out as many unknowns as I can, if possible, because once I know what to expect I can approach it in an appropriate way. If there are sections which are not well protected or where I am not allowed to fall I assess whether it is worth the risk for me, and once I have decided to go for it I switch my brain off to the danger, focusing only on the climbing, on every individual movement being accurate and fluid. If I am on an on-sight, without any prior knowledge of the climb, I will do this assessment continually throughout the route. However, the actual process is still the same.

For me the process for mentally preparing for a hard trad route or hard redpoint is very similar. Over the weeks prior to my attempt, I visualise in detail me climbing the route. This is not simply visualising the movements, but also the way each hold will feel under my fingers and how I will feel while climbing (my emotional state) so that by the time I actually go to get on the route I have basically climbed it many times in my head. I try to make it feel the way it would if I really have to fight for the route.

The day of the attempt I try to just run through my normal routine. Not putting extra pressure on myself is very key for me. Often I know I only have one shot, but I find it important to keep telling myself that it doesn't matter if I send or not, just to give it everything and that as long as I give my very best effort then the outcome doesn't matter. This approach removes a little of the pressure that I often put on myself and allows me to climb in a freer state of mind – letting my body follow its own flow.

Right before I get on the rock I take a few minutes to be still, breathe deeply, clear my head and centre myself. The technique that works well for me is focusing on my breath and thinking of a place or time that puts me in a peaceful state and removing any unnecessary concerns or thoughts from my brain, so that I can pull on to the rock focusing purely on the moment. Sometimes I try to remember the state or feeling I have had from previous significant sends, thereby elevating my mental senses and priming myself for the send ...

Like I mentioned above, I feel like the mental state I use has similarities, however when mentally preparing for a trad line that is either scary, run out or dangerous, I find I want to start climbing in a calmer and more totally focused state. This is often also the best state for a hard sport route, however when there is no risk I often do not put as much emphasis on making sure I am in that state because there is no consequence, apart from not sending (of course).

Also I feel that trad climbing is a more personal adventure. Unless there are very limited gear placements, you can choose where and how much protection you place, how good it is and make your own decision of what you choose to trust. While sport climbing you have bolts that have been placed by someone else and you just need to choose whether you trust them or not.

For these reasons I also feel that the role that your mind plays is higher in hard trad climbing than sport climbing. It requires more mental control to make physically hard movements when you do not have a fixed piece of gear to aim for, or need to save the energy to place gear. Additionally it is simply more complex – you have to pull more factors together than in sport climbing and there are more things that can go wrong.

One of my strengths is being able to shut out the entire world when on a hard climb. While I am in a good climbing mind space I focus only on the climb and do not hear or register anything else that is going on around me.

I find some external pressure helps to make me function at my best, but I need to be aware to not put much pressure on myself. To give it everything without focusing or putting pressure on the outcome. If I am too anxious about the outcome I tend to overthink things, causing myself to climb in a tense state and not let my body simply flow. If I can shut off that side of my brain it enables me to let my body move freely and more efficiently.

MAYAN
SMITH-GOBAT

In the past, I often sent my hardest redpoints third or fourth try of the day when my body is tired and I have given up hope of sending, letting me relax and let this flow happen.'

So that's it: my experience, that of world-renowned Professor Lew Hardy who has specialised in elite sports for around forty years and with the climbers' contributions, who have reached the pinnacle of our sport, combined, is over a hundred years of experience. Now it's over to you.

It's a cliché to say that no two people are the same, but it's also true. In the context of this book, some will read this book once, take away the highlights and enjoy the inspirational stories. Others will use the book actively, reading it again and again over the years, as a way of achieving more from their climbing and doing progressively harder routes. Of course, both are fine.

The people that use the book actively are likely to be as obsessive about their climbing as I was. I hope the ideas that I and others have shared will be a way of channelling that obsession so that you achieve an optimum performance on any given day and that, over time, you achieve your maximum potential and enjoyment in your climbing. As I said at the start, when I was younger I thought it was all about strength and power and climbing all day, every day. However, we know that getting the most out of your climbing essentially depends on getting your mind in the right place to allow you to perform. When you can do that you're capable of succeeding under pressure in any situation. This will give you those memorable days that I can only describe as euphoric and perfect.

In order to perform at a high level, there are a lot of things you have to get right. It is not easy and that is why people struggle. Processes can go wrong and you have to get them right. Things like having appropriate goals, being able to concentrate, staying in the present, focusing on things that are important, inhibiting things that are not relevant, being physically fit, warming up properly, thinking positively about the event, skin, weather conditions, etc, etc.

Bank your success. There is no question that if you are more confident, it will have a positive impact on your climbing. For optimum performance, the task has to be very challenging. You need pressure and anxiety to make you really concentrate. Don't get me wrong, these are not the nicest feelings. I don't particularly like feeling scared or anxious either. You need it, but at the same time you need to be able to control it. Early preparation is vital. Be positively cautious, looking for all the things that could go wrong, and work out how you would react. It is rare that everything goes perfectly so those anti-goals need to be picked up and then inhibited. The more you can narrow your focus down to one process goal the more you will be able to concentrate. What is the singular thing that if you do right will get you up the piece of rock in front of you? Make that your process goal, focus on that then trust your unconscious skills to do the rest.

One of the differences between climbing and other sports is that you often go into complete muscle failure. You're totally pumped at the top of a route, the lactic acid hits, everything hurts, your fingers open and you're off. The climbs you will remember for the rest of your life are the ones where you are pushing those physical and mental limits to the maximum. Be strong, robust, forceful and ready for a fight.

■ ∎ ■

Embrace that battle of holding it together when you're pumped out of your brain slapping for the top. Commit yourself, don't let go, hang in there, do whatever it takes to get that next hold. Be inspired.

Be inspired
now it's over to
you

Jerry's message

© Hannes Huch

II

INSPIRATIONAL STORIES:

'IF MY MIND CAN CONCEIVE IT
AND MY HEART CAN BELIEVE IT,
THEN I CAN ACHIEVE IT.'
MUHAMMAD ALI

INSPIRATIONAL STORIES

'IT'S EASY TO GET "SUMMIT FEVER" – THAT'S WHAT MY DAD CALLS IT. YOU GET CLOSE TO THE TOP AND YOU WANT IT SO BADLY THAT YOU LOSE FOCUS. SO IT'S IMPORTANT TO BREATHE AND FOCUS ON EACH MOVE.'

Margo Hayes
climbing
La Rambla (F9a+)

© Greg Mionske

ADAM ONDRA

LA DURA DURA

La Dura Dura – that was the hardest psychological procedure I've had with a route and the longest. In all it took nine weeks, spread over five different trips. The year I did it felt like I spent more time in Spain than at home. I've tried the route just so many times; it's just like the hardest route in the world.

I think it really helps that I did not live near the route. You can clearly cut the training phases and the phases on your project. When I went back home I was not distracted, like, maybe I can try it today and see how it is. Now I can just train then when I arrive back to the route I think, 'Now it's time to try.' Living near the route like Chris it's so easy to get distracted and not to train actually.

On my first trip I was thinking the route is hard but maybe I can do with a few more weeks. Looking back retrospectively I was nowhere close. I was way too weak to send it because working on a certain route I would say after two weeks that you've got the route so wired that you either send it in a few days or it's better to leave it, train and get even stronger.

So for me that was always the hope that if I can't do it this time I can go away and train harder and come back super excited. I went away, trained harder and came back stronger, but that may have only got me one move higher! On *La Dura Dura* it was like this; every single time before I went back to it I was feeling super strong. I was thinking this progression will be finally enough to send it, but no. I still had to progress way more than I expected. Sometimes let's say I went for a two-week trip, after a week I found out I had made some progression but it's not going to be enough. So in that case I was pretty negative, but overall there was hope that I will do it one day, let's say in a year. The hope was still there because I can still see progression. If I couldn't see the progression, if I was getting further and further away from my goal I would probably get frustrated and leave it for a year.

ADAM ONDRA + BORN 1993 IN THE CZECH REPUBLIC + ARGUABLY BEST CLIMBER IN THE WORLD + HE OPENED THE FIRST F9C IN 2017 *SILENCE* IN NORWAY + ON-SIGHTED SEVERAL F9A + FLASHED BOULDERS UP TO FONT 8B+ + 2014 WORLD CHAMPION BOULDER AND LEAD + REPEATED THE *DAWN WALL* IN JUST TWO WEEKS

Because there was this tiny continuous progression that was the key for me. It doesn't have to necessarily be every time you try it you make a high point.

It can be that I might have fallen one move earlier, but there I was feeling a little bit stronger and today the conditions are a little worse.

You have to pick something good and it does not necessarily have to be true. The most important thing is that your mind believes it, you can lie to your mind; if you think something positive and your mind believes it then that's good enough.

Sometimes lying to your mind is very good, for instance you have to take conditions into consideration; that's very wise to pick something positive.

On a route like *La Dura Dura* I don't always think this try is going to be the send. My goal of the try might be that I want to make the high point. It's pretty obvious the first two or three weeks that you just can't do it; you just want to feel something. Every single day was a little sparkle of hope. Even warming up on a 7c+ the way to trick my mind was, 'Oh this feels so easy', even if it might not have been true, but if it helped me to perform better on *La Dura Dura* then it worked. The first trip I had in February was fun. I kept trying and made slight progression. Then in March, hoping maybe that I could even send it, that trip was really frustrating because I made some progression but it was less than I expected. In April I was feeling super strong and I was super confident that I could do it, but I only had five days. And that time if I had one week more then maybe I could send it. Then I returned in December thinking now I am even stronger but I just forgot the route so I just started from the beginning.

I finally found out I have the route so wired that it doesn't feel any easier; there is no margin to make anything more efficient. My muscles just memorised the moves so perfectly I either need to be just a little bit stronger or have more luck.

Then for my fifth trip actually from the first day I knew I could do it. That was a situation because in that moment I knew I could do it any day. I fell two or three times from the last hard move; maybe even one fall was a little stupid.

In the process of trying a route for so long one moment arrives when you say, 'Okay this is the moment I know I can do it and I should do it.'

There is a moment when you just know and hopefully the conditions will stick. On *La Dura Dura* the moment I realised I was going to send it was three days before I sent it. I was pretty proud that these last three days my confidence was just so so good. Yes I did fall, I got super frustrated, but looking at the forecast which was perfect for another week I was like, 'It doesn't really matter, I know I can do it.'

When I finally stuck the crux I couldn't have been really any closer to falling, then as I was resting I felt like I would have a heart attack, it was so intense, so hard to calm down.

The top could be 8b by itself; it was just really sketchy because I just really didn't want to mess it up. After trying this route for nine weeks falling off the very very top would really suck. I was lucky enough to send the route after ten days on that trip.

What do I say, how do I describe how happy I was?

I had an empty mind, no worries and I just did everything perfectly.

My dream came true. Thanks, Chris, for bolting this beast!

■ ■ ■

Adam Ondra
climbing *La Dura
Dura* (F9b+)

© Bernado
Gimenez

JERRY MOFFATT

BEST BIRTHDAY

It was the winter of 1984 and one of my best mates, Andy Pollitt, had just returned from an all-expenses-paid British Mountaineering Council trip to France.

Up until that point I had spent two weeks in Fontainebleau, but never done any routes there; I was super keen to go.

Andy spent the last few days of the meet at a cliff called Le Saussois, which is a few hours' drive south of Fontainebleau.

The cliff sounded really cool – smooth white limestone covered in pockets, quite short and powerful, which I really liked.

Kim Carrigan, Ron Fawcett, Wolfgang Krauss and Patrick Edlinger were some of the climbers on the meet and all world-class at that time. They had all been trying a route called *Chimpanzodrome* which was graded F7c+. It was done by Jean-Pierre Bouvier in 1981 and was one of the first 7c+s. I also completed the first pitch of *Rooster Booster* that year which is also 7c+. Who knows which was first?

I think they all tried it at the meet, but only had a day on it and all failed. It really got my fire and competitiveness burning. I got it into my head that I was going to flash it. I hadn't flashed anything of that grade up to that point, in fact no one had, but I had on-sighted 7c. It's funny, back then in England there was no such thing as 'on-sight'. You just tried to do something without falls. If your mate was there and knew how to do it, of course you would ask him how to do it, why not?

It was a great goal – to try and flash one of France's hardest routes. It made all the training that winter so much easier. Although it was pre-climbing walls, we did have a finger edge to do pull-ups on and a few machines to do weights. There was also the side of the Sheffield University building for traversing, which was about eight metres by three metres and had a little balcony above it so it always stayed dry. The wall was made up of hard sand blocks covered in edges which we made up some great eliminate traverses on. That was how we spent the winter: pull-ups, hangs and traversing then pull-ups, hangs in the afternoon. For rest, we played table tennis and cards. I spent all my time at the university. Fortunately, no one ever asked if was a student! This was before sponsorship, and I got my money from the government because I was unemployed.

It was a great time. No one had any money, but no one had the stress or worries either. There were about eight of us all living in one house, all climbers and all unemployed. I didn't actually rent a room in the house, but very kindly my mate Tim and his girlfriend Mandy let me sleep on the floor.

Also staying there was a very young seventeen-year-old Ben Moon who I had met in Wales. I told him to come to Sheffield and spend the winter training. He was super keen and a great training partner. He hadn't done anything hard up until that point – I think 7b.

At the end of March, we set off for a two-month climbing trip to France. We didn't have a car so went lightweight, as we were going to have to hitch-hike everywhere. We didn't bring a tent or cooker either, as there wasn't much room in our backpacks.

After a couple of days in a freezing Fontainebleau, we hitchhiked down to Le Saussois.

The cliff was amazing, although the reality of staying there was pretty grim. There were no shops nearby to buy bread and nowhere to hang out. It was an hour walk in the morning each way just to get bread. When it got dark in the evening we got into our sleeping bags and just listened to music on the Walkman.

There had been a new route done over the winter called *Bidule*; it was grade F8a+ and the hardest route in France at the time. I jumped straight on it and Ben set to work on *Chimpanzodrome*. It was very convenient as both routes were next to each other. We were both successful after three days. It was a great effort from Ben as his previous hardest climb had only been about 7b. Having belayed Ben, I got a good look at the moves of *Chimpanzodrome* and tried to memorise them.

I had dreamt all winter of flashing this route and doing it wouldn't have been a problem; I was quite sure the only challenge was the flash.

My birthday was 18 March which was in two days' time, and it was also to be my twenty-first. We didn't really have rest days back then, but I decided to have a rest day so I could try it on my twenty-first birthday. It was all or nothing!

The big day arrived. It was a Sunday. Up until that point we hadn't seen any climbers, but because it was the weekend quite a few cars turned up with climbers. We were in our sleeping bags dossing under an overhang at the base of the route called *L'Ange*. We must have looked a sight. I did a 7b overhang for a warm-up, then went to the base of *Chimpanzodrome*. I was just so psyched! I decided to lead it on a single 8.5mm. I also climbed in just a belt with no leg loops to keep the weight down. I wore my lucky vest; it was a T-shirt with the arms cut off with a picture of a parrot on it with 'Venezuela' written underneath. My dad had bought it for me on returning from a business trip there (I still have it).

I was ready. I don't remember much about the climb, except I felt really strong; absolutely nothing was going to stop me flashing it.

I smoked the crux then ran it out to the last bolt, clipped it super quick and powered past. Ben was shouting something. I looked down to the bolt at my feet. I realised that in my haste I hadn't clipped the bolt. It was a little alarming, as I was looking at a ground fall. Although the climbing was still hard, I managed to reach down and re-clip the bolt. All that training had paid off; I was just so happy. I had given myself just the best birthday present ever. Who needs cards, presents and a party?! After that we went over to *L'Ange*, a three-pitch 7b and a classic which I also on-sighted. What a day. We had ticked the crag.

With nothing really left to do there, we put our stuff in our rucksacks and decided to start the long hitch down to our next destination, Buoux in the south. One of the local French climbers picked us up and dropped us at the toll on the autoroute. It was about six o'clock and dense freezing fog. After about a couple of hours waiting it was clear we were not going to get a lift. We got our sleeping bags out and dossed down next to the motorway. It was noisy and freezing, not really the way most people spend their twenty-first birthday. I lay there and went to sleep with a smile on my face.

It was the best birthday ever!

ANNA STÖHR

MEADOWLARK LEMON

When it comes down to the hard boulder problems it's kind of difficult for me to tell which ones I can actually climb.

I'm only 1.63 metres, not exactly tall, and my ape index is just +2. So I have to assess carefully which boulder problems I can do with my limited wingspan. Many boulders require moves that are simply too reachy for me. I don't always chase high grades, but sometimes I get curious to see what I can achieve, difficulty-wise.

It was like that in Las Vegas where we started off with two really good days. On the first day the sun was shining, but we were really jetlagged from the flight. On day two I wanted to check out *Meadowlark Lemon* (Font 8b), so we hiked over there. I once saw Paul Robinson climb it and I thought, 'Wow, that's a real beauty of a boulder! Those red and white lines – awesome!' I could reach all the holds, and it actually went quite well. Not bad for a start. But then it began to rain, and for the next eight days we couldn't get any climbing done. Killing so much time in Vegas was really tedious. After a while all I wanted to do was climb, I was so psyched for this boulder. As a professional climber I am used to climbing almost all the time, so a forced break like this one felt really awkward.

My motivation increased dramatically, and getting on the rock was all I wanted. When it finally stopped raining we went straight to *Meadowlark*. I managed to do all the moves which was the goal for the day. There was plenty of time left so I made a few attempts and surprisingly it went really well. I fell two times at the crux and thought, 'Cool, I can climb this!' On my next attempt, I reached the slab. Yeah, I got it?! I reached for the jug and ... suddenly found myself on the pad below ('on me', adds Kilian who is sitting next to Anna).

I became very pessimistic because the skin on my fingertips was gone and I was totally knackered. Nevertheless I did try a couple more times until it got dark. I couldn't stick the crux anyway. I was really angry, but I also knew I could do it. I just needed some patience. That wasn't easy for me though because I'm a total anti-project climber. If I attempt a boulder for three days, I'm already at my

ANNA STÖHR + BORN 1988 IN AUSTRIA + MOST SUCCESSFUL FEMALE COMPETITION BOULDERER WON THE WORLD CUP FOUR TIMES + MULTIPLE WORLD AND EUROPEAN CHAMPION + SHE REPEATED BOULDERS UP TO FONT 8B+ + HARDEST BOULDER *NEW BASE LINE* (FONT 8B+)

limit of patience. The next day, we went there again because I felt quite well. But I also had doubts. Was my skin too thin? Was it too warm?

Well, sometimes you just have to stop whining, get a grip and push it to the max. And even if you know that it's possible you still have to concentrate on every move.

And that's how I did *Meadowlark Lemon*.

Anna Stöhr
sending
*Meadowlark
Lemon* (Font 8b)

© Kilian
Fischhuber

ALEX MEGOS

LUCID DREAMING – WHY THIS ONE?

What am I doing? What am I thinking? I just booked a plane ticket to LA to try three stupid moves on some boulder in the middle of the desert. Why??!!

The answer is easy and simple. Because I want to climb those three moves, in one piece. But why is this so important to me? There are so many things out there to choose from, does it have to be this one? Does it have to be *Lucid Dreaming* (Font 8c) in the Buttermilks near Bishop, California, which are around 9,000 kilometres away from my home? Yes! It has to be exactly this one. It has to be this one because I want to prove to myself that I can do it, that I am capable of climbing it.

I first tried *Lucid Dreaming* in November 2014. I still had five days left on my trip and I thought, 'Let's see what happens if I dedicate all five days to one boulder problem.' Day one went quite well. I stuck the third move, the jump to the crimp, which is supposed to be the hardest out of the three moves. On day two, I pretty much pieced together the beta for the first two moves. On day three, I still couldn't link two moves. On the fourth day, I couldn't do any of the moves any more. On day five, I gave up and went bouldering to enjoy the last day of my trip. In my eyes, I had failed, actually for the first time in my life (on a climb, that is).

It was the first time I really wanted to climb something but couldn't do it, and that absolutely drove me crazy. I was thinking about it all the time. It wouldn't leave me alone.

So there was just one way out: fly back for those three moves and do them!

Of course I wanted to be prepared this time, I didn't want anything to go wrong. A good friend of mine, Peter, made the crux pinch of the climb out of wood and gave it to me as a Christmas present. I also built a replica of the last move on the 45er in Café Kraft straight

ALEX MEGOS + BORN 1993 IN GERMANY + WELL KNOWN FOR FAST REPETITIONS OF THE HARDEST ROUTES + STUNNED CLIMBING SCENE BY REPEATING *ACTION DIRECTE* (F9A) WITHIN JUST TWO HOURS + *BIOGRAPHIE* (F9A+) IN A DAY + 2013 WORLD'S FIRST F9A ON-SIGHT – *ESTADO CRITICO* IN SIURANA + SINCE THEN HE HAS ALMOST DONE EVERYTHING HE HAS LAID HIS HANDS ON + THE BOULDER *LUCID DREAMING* IS HIS HARDEST BOULDER TO DATE

The wooden replica of the crux pinch of *Lucid Dreaming* in the Café Kraft gym.

© Hannes Huch

away. I trained on it for ten days straight till I did ten out of ten jumps on my last day before departure. I was confident that nothing could go wrong. I would get there and just walk it – piece of cake.

I got there and it was devastating, depressing and simply pathetic. I couldn't do the jump move on the original for the whole day. That brought me back down to earth. I realised again that it was hard and it wouldn't be a walk in the park. On day two, I started to make some progress; I stuck the jump move. On day three, I did the bottom moves again. On day six, I still couldn't link two moves, but I felt ready to give it some tries so I took a rest day.

It wasn't until day seven that I began to feel confident from the start, knowing that I could do it. I got very close that day, fell during the jump move a couple of times, almost holding the swing. The sun came in though at some point and I decided to call it a day. Just one last try, after I actually had already called it a day. Why does the last try always have to be the bad one? I split three tips in one try! What followed was the first and only time during a trip till now that I rested two days in a row. People tried to convince me to even take a third one, but I couldn't! I had to go back and try again.

That morning, the morning of the eighth day, it was foggy and rainy. I superglued all the tape to my fingers to make sure it wouldn't slip.

The first time I touched the pinch during my warm-up routine I knew today was the day.

On my second try that day I pieced it together and it felt smooth and effortless. Not even the fifteen-metre-high wet slab would stop me any more. With the help of a chalk bag that was thrown up to me I dried the holds and finally stood on top of Grandpa Peabody. The feeling was one of the best things I've ever experienced in my life. You can't describe the satisfaction you get out of it to anybody who hasn't felt the same. You feel so happy deep down in your heart, a feeling that you don't get very often in life. Those are the moments I climb for. Those are the moments all the effort pays off.

■— ■ —■

JIMMY WEBB

LIVIN' LARGE

My biggest achievement mentally was doing Nalle's boulder problem *Livin' Large* in South Africa. It's by far the best experience that I've had in climbing.

I worked the hell out of it one season, then at one point I suddenly realised I had just three weeks left. The problem is so sharp I had to take mini rest days. So I had to try it in the morning, get up super early, then rest the whole rest of the day, all the next day and then wake up at 5 a.m. the next day and do it again. I counted down the days. So three weeks left made eight more days on it. Then you're trying it, and rest, and trying it, and rest ... five more days, four more days, three more days ... and then it got down to THE last day. The very last day of my trip. The pressure was absolutely immense. Again the same experience: woke up at 5 a.m., at the wall on the rope doing the top moves with a head lamp. It was super intense, because I had been up there fourteen days this trip. I had seven pads which is prob- ably not quite enough for that climb, pretty bad pads too. Then on this very last day of my trip the sun started to rise, the light just came up, then up the hill walks Nalle! The only day he'd been up there with me and he brought a huge Mondo pad. He arrived right when I was up to give it a burn; he laid the pad down for me and spotted.

Something like superhuman strength suddenly occurred and I climbed it.

First ascent for him, second ascent for me and he was there to watch it, to spot and to be there. No words can fully describe the feeling I had when I stuck the final jug. I rushed down the hill to the cabins where we stayed and everybody was super psyched then there was something like a party. I didn't have long; I jumped straight in the car and headed to the airport to get my plane back home. Such a good feeling, man!

— ∎ —

JIMMY WEBB + BORN 1987 IN THE USA + CONSIDERED THE 'WORLD'S BEST FLASH BOULDERER' + FLASHED SIX FONT 8B OR HARDER BOULDER PROBLEMS + REPEATED AND OPENED MANY OF THE WORLD'S HARDEST BOULDER PROBLEMS LIKE *EPHYRA* (FONT 8C+), SWITZERLAND + REPEATED THE HIGHBALL *LIVIN' LARGE* (FONT 8C)

Jimmy Webb
climbing *Livin'
Large* (Font 8c)

© Carlo Traversi

KILIAN FISCHHUBER

VICTORY IN VAIL

The event in Vail, Colorado, was the first Boulder World Cup in the States back in 2006. There was such a big crowd and everyone seemed to expect that the Americans would win.

But it turned out that it came down to Gabri Moroni and me in the finals. On the very last boulder Gabri started first and he did the problem second try. I came last and I knew I had just one try. I actually had to flash the boulder to win, which was highly unlikely. Only Gabri was able to send the problem up until then. All the others had failed. I just concentrated on climbing and ignored the commentator who was all about 'Kilian has to flash this boulder, he has just one try' and so on. That's how you create a lot of suspense for the audience, but it also put a lot of pressure on me, obviously. Surprisingly, it unleashed a lot of power that I might not have had in a usual go.

Even though it was a very long boulder, I didn't have much time to think. I did one move, second move, one after the other ... and then I faced the last hold. It was really far away. Again, it was highly unlikely that I would stick. But then I went for it, made a huge swing, matched hands and therefore flashed the boulder and won the World Cup. That was really special and the victory meant a lot to me.

When you can flash the last boulder in a competition, when you have only one try left – you grow a lot. The thing is that you have to believe in it. You can't say it was just luck. You have to make this your strength.

You have to transform something that went well into something you can believe in.

It helped me a lot over the years. Because I can always remember that it worked back then and I'm sure it will work out again. When you have a long career and a lot of success you can slowly fill your own box of positive moments and develop your own strategy to do so. But you have to pick your memories wisely – focus only on the positive aspects.

— ∎ —

KILIAN FISCHHUBER + BORN 1983 IN AUSTRIA + VERY SUCCESSFUL IN THE BOULDER WORLD CUP CIRCUIT FOR OVER A DECADE + FIVE TIMES OVERALL BOULDERING WORLD CUP WINNER + EUROPEAN CHAMPION + ARCO ROCK MASTER BOULDERING + REPEATED *ACTION DIRECTE* (F9A) + REPEATED THE BOULDER *FROM DIRT GROWS THE FLOWERS* (FONT 8C) AND MANY MORE

'YOU HAVE TO TRANS-
FORM SOMETHING
THAT WENT WELL INTO
SOMETHING YOU CAN
BELIEVE IN.'

Kilian Fischhuber

© Hannes Huch

LENA HERRMANN

Lena Herrmann climbing *Klondike Cat* (F8c)

© Rico Haase

LENA HERRMANN + BORN 1994 + ONE OF THE STRONGEST CLIMBERS IN GERMANY + SENDING *BATTLE CAT* (F8C+) MADE HER THE FIRST GERMAN WOMAN TO CLIMB A ROUTE OF THAT GRADE

THE POWER OF EMOTIONS

My dad was the most faithful climbing partner and supporter during most of my life. His encouragement was crucial, as I often lacked confidence to take up a real challenge.

I couldn't even imagine climbing what my dad thought I could climb one day. I already had a hunch what would eventually happen in 2015, but I had no idea how much it would collide with my most difficult ascent to date. My dad and I were dreaming about the lower eleventh grade. Of course I was the one who would actually do the climbing, but nowadays I realise how much he contributed to my success. As my loyal companion he tenderly scrubbed holds, made me sandwiches and chauffeured me around. All my redpoint ascents were a team effort.

At that time, *Klondike Cat* was my hardest project so far, and the first one where my dad could only be with me on the phone due to his poor health. When I was told that he wouldn't have much longer to live I knew I had exactly one chance to make our little dream about the eleventh grade come true. I was at the Franconian Jura that day. Of course I was thinking mostly about the bad news and how to cope. I had decided to stay another day and not to go home immediately, as I felt safe and comfortable among my friends. My first few tries were as bad as never before. It was incredibly hot, it was crowded there, and my thoughts were somewhere else entirely. Nevertheless I kept trying, and eventually had one of those rare flow experiences. It always feels like magically being carried to the top.

Today I'm still convinced that sending *Klondike Cat* on exactly that day was due to my desire to tell my dad and see the pride in his eyes one last time. It's also why I think that no matter how dutifully we train, no matter how well-structured our training is,

it's always the things we can't control that have the greatest effect on our performance.

Whether it's unconditional support from our parents, the sometimes crucial advice from a coach or the generous amount of time that our friends spend while belaying and keeping us safe, climbing has taught me how important it is to be grateful.

CHRIS SHARMA

ALASHA

Aside from all my hard redpoints my best days' climbing have been soloing these deep-water solo projects. I recently did a route called *Alasha*, named after my daughter Alana Sharma.

For me this was a super-epic project, just a super-beautiful line. It's like doing an 8b boulder at fifteen to eighteen metres above the sea.

I was just there with my buddy Ricardo who was taking pictures and videoing. He had a flotation device in case something happened. He was literally hanging out on the ropes above and I was in the cave below. Just sitting in the cave looking out at the horizon, just the Mediterranean Sea with the waves crashing. I was just zoning out and kind of focusing my energy. I just went up and executed everything perfectly, super-low-percentage moves. I was just hitting them perfectly. It's very intense because you're doing super-hard moves when you just feel like you could explode off in super-crazy positions into the ocean. It's a really exposed location; deep water and cliff line for miles. It's not like other locations when you have sandy beaches nearby; at this place you're just in the elements.

I did it and it was just absolutely freaking epic!

I've had so many amazing days of climbing and moments, climbing *La Dura Dura*, *Jumbo Love*, *First Round First Minute*, *Biographie*. All these routes are super important and were perfect days. When you achieve something like that they are just perfect moments in climbing.

Everything clicks and your mind and body are in the right place.

Your body is super-fine-tuned, you are as fit as you've ever been and your mind is working along with your body. The conditions are right and they are perfect moments in our lives. So any of those particular routes are perfect moments in climbing, don't you think?

— ∎ —

CHRIS SHARMA + BORN 1981 IN THE USA + MOST FAMOUS AMBASSADOR OF CLIMBING + DID THE HARDEST ROUTE IN THE STATES *NECESSARY EVIL* AT AGE OF FIFTEEN + OPENED THE FIRST F9A+ *REALIZATION* AND F9B *JUMBO LOVE* + DEEP WATER SOLOING HIGHLIGHT WAS *ES PONTAS* F9B ON MALLORCA + ONLY PERSON BESIDES ADAM ONDRA WHO HAS CLIMBED *LA DURA DURA*

Chris Sharma on
Alasha (F8b)

© Ricardo
Giancola

STEFAN GLOWACZ

PUNKS IN THE GYM

Punks in the Gym was a hard fight because it was way too hot.

I had to get up at 4 a.m. to be at the rock one hour later just when the sun came up. That was such hard work, but I really wanted to climb that route before I went home. When I looked at my flight schedule I felt under huge pressure. So the whole situation was kind of wrong. It was way too hot. I had to climb early in the morning because in the evening in the shade the rock was too hot to climb on and I'm really not an early-bird climber. So I had to get used to getting up at 4 a.m., that's why I did that on my rest days as well.

Especially in the morning I visualised all the moves intensely because I wanted to do *Punks* so badly.

This mental preparation was the key to doing it some days later. Even if everything is wrong and against you, the confidence that you can do it nevertheless is essential. Even if the chances are very small you have to believe in yourself.

— ▪ —

STEFAN GLOWACZ + BORN 1965 + PROBABLY FIRST SPECIALIST COMPETITION CLIMBER + MULTIPLE ARCO ROCK MASTER + DID SEVERAL TOUGH FIRST ASCENTS IN REMOTE AREAS SUCH AS BAFFIN ISLAND OR VENEZUELA + OPENED SERIOUS MULTI-PITCH ROUTES IN THE ALPS + SECOND REPEAT OF WOLFGANG GÜLLICH'S *PUNKS IN THE GYM* 8B

Jerry climbing
Punks in the Gym
(F8b+)

© Glenn Robbins

BEN MOON

RAINSHADOW FOURTH ASCENT

I finally realised the dream I had of climbing Steve McClure's classic 9a route *Rainshadow* on 8 June 2015. The dream began while walking in the Yorkshire Dales with my wife in 2012.

Our route took us under the amazing limestone cove of Malham. It wasn't a great day for climbing, most of the cove was wet, but there was one lone climber working a route up the centre of the cove. It turned out to be Jordan Buys, and the route was *Rainshadow*. At the time, I knew little or nothing about the route other than it was one of the hardest in the UK and graded 9a. Adam Ondra repeated it in 2011 in just two days, and afterwards he said it was one of the best 9a routes he had climbed. Later, in 2012, Jordan made the third ascent.

Since that day, I've learnt a lot more about this route and what makes it so special. It takes a stunning line up the centre of the cove on bullet-hard limestone and requires that special combination of strength and endurance. It's not enough to be either strong or fit, you need to be strong and fit. The route starts up a classic 8a called *Raindogs* before trending right below the huge crux bulge to a poor resting spot. To this point it is Font 8a+. After the rest, you make a couple of moves up to the bulge before the meat of the route instantly kicks in, a twelve-move Font 8a boulder problem on poor pinches, layaways and underclings. Once you have negotiated this there is no time to rest or catch your breath before launching out left to find your way up the impending headwall at Font 8a+. It's a stunning climb in an impressive location and a must-climb 9a route.

After a really hard winter of training at the newly built School Room, I headed up to Malham on 10 February for my first attempt. I expected it to be a very long campaign. My experience of 9a is pretty much limited to *Hubble*, *Action Directe* and my Kilnsey project *Northern Lights* and I didn't really know what to expect. I was initially quite shocked at the difficulty of the boulder problem and although I did manage it in two overlapping sections I couldn't imagine climbing it after doing an 8a+ route. Leaving the crag that day I was preparing myself for a long battle over two or three seasons.

BEN MOON + BORN 1966 IN THE UK + OPENED *HUBBLE* , WORLD'S FIRST F8C+ ROUTE IN 1990 + DID MANY HARD BOULDER PROBLEMS BEFORE THE TIME OF CRASH PADS LIKE *THE THING* (FONT 8A+) IN 1987 + MOTIVATED A WHOLE GENERATION AGAIN WITH HIS REPEAT OF *RAINSHADOW* AT THE AGE OF FORTY-NINE

Over the next two months, I continued my training interspersed with regular trips to Malham to work the three sections that make up *Rainshadow*. By day five, I had climbed the crux sequence in a oner and by day seven, I had climbed the crux sequence to the top. With the benefit of hard training and a good strategy, the route had come together a lot quicker than I expected. My diary entry for 17 April ended with the words 'Need to start redpointing'. Working routes is great fun, but redpointing them is a serious, high-pressure business. The harder the route, the more time invested, the higher the pressure.

Dealing with this pressure is what hard redpointing is all about – and you have to embrace it.

I cut out all my training and everything was geared around two weekly trips to Malham and making sure I was in peak condition for these two days. My expectations were high because of the links I had done while working the route, but there is some stuff you just cannot learn about a route until you start redpointing. During the working phase, I had broken the route down into sections and I took the same approach on redpointing. Each day I made progress, but still couldn't get through the boulder problem crux. Suddenly, on day fifteen I made it through the crux, but immediately powered out without making the slightest impact on the 8a+ headwall. Suddenly, doubt crept in and I questioned whether I was fit enough for the route. Then the unbelievable happened and on the last go of the day I was through the crux a second time and feeling good. No time to think, just go, and before I knew it I was through the top crux of the 8a+ headwall and looking at the last hard move. I threw for the layaway, my fingers curled around it, but I couldn't hold on and the next moment I was flying through the air and the dream was over! I couldn't believe I had fallen off.

It was half term now and I had promised my family we would do family stuff together and I wouldn't go to Malham. I had ten days to think about my failure and to live with the expectation from within myself and from all my friends who thought the route was now a dead cert. With this level of expectation, I was never going to do it on my next day. Although I again got high on the headwall I was totally pumped. I had been climbing a lot with Steve McClure and in my moments of doubt he gave me the confidence to believe I was good enough. He told me that today simply wasn't the day, but that it would come for sure. When I started the redpoint phase, I gave myself six weeks to complete the route. If it didn't happen, I would walk away and come back another time. My six weeks were almost up and I had just two more redpoint days before the walk away. Day eighteen seemed just like the other days, although my first redpoint attempt was worse than on previous days. I battled through the crux boulder problem, but immediately powered out and made no impact on the 8a+ headwall. Time was running out. I walked up the hill next to the cove thinking about Sharma's words as he battled with the pressure to redpoint *Biographie*, the world's first 9a+: 'Everything has to come together perfectly for me to do this route ... feel strong, but not too confident. Have the desire to do it, but not too attached on getting to the top as much as just enjoying the climbing.'

I lay down in the sun, closed my eyes and went slowly through the sixty-move sequence that would take me to the top. Near the top of the route I could feel myself drifting off, but managed to bring myself back to clip the chains before letting myself go completely.

One hour later I awoke from my sleep, walked back down the hill, tied in and redpointed *Rainshadow*. I felt great, strong through the crux, slightly pumped on the top section but always in control. I really couldn't believe it. The best and hardest route I've ever done? Yes, definitely. I feel incredibly lucky to have found climbing, and as I get older I can see and appreciate this more than ever.

BEN MOON

'LIFE IS VERY PRECIOUS. LIVE HEALTHY, TRAIN HARD, CLIMB HARDER.'

PETE WHITTAKER

SOLO-FREE IN TWENTY-FOUR HOURS

Three in the afternoon. I stand at the base of *Free-rider* on El Cap. Just 'Mike' by my side, ready to free-climb the entire granite monolith in a single twenty-four-hour push, alone.

There will be nobody to split the load with, nobody to draw motivation from, nobody to help problem-solve and nobody to be on hand in the event of an accident. Everything will be down to me, which will be brutal, but at the end all the work will have been mine and I can be content with that.

I am physically, mentally, technically and logistically prepared.

I know it is going to be a fight and a challenge, maybe the hardest challenge I've tried doing, but that's what I am looking for. So, when I step off the ground, I am ready.

Halfway up the initial pitch, those feelings of nervousness, excitement and adrenaline all channel into my climbing, and I can feel I am moving well and without the fear I'd had before setting off. Long run-outs that were made to speed up my movement melt below me into a blur. I am incredibly surprised when I check the watch after the first eleven pitches to find I've done them in under three hours and thirty minutes, however I have only done the easy part of the wall. I still have all the cruxes to come.

At half height, I've covered one of the four cruxes and by this point my body can feel it. It is 1 a.m., I feel like going to sleep, I have stomach cramps from trying to eat while constantly exerting energy and my muscles are starting to tire from double the amount of work I have to do compared to climbing with a partner.

I am exhausted, feel like stopping, but I don't have time for that, I have to stick to my rhythm: climb, tend device, climb, tend device, climb, fix rope, abseil, retrieve bag, jumar, clean gear, repeat. It becomes a mantra.

PETE WHITTAKER + BORN 1992 + SPECIALISES IN TRAD CLIMBING AND CRACK CLIMBING + REALISED GROUNDBREAKING ASCENTS LIKE *CENTURY CRACK* (5.14B) IN 2011 + ALL FREE ROPE SOLO ASCENT OF *FREERIDER* ON EL CAPITAN, YOSEMITE

Pete Whittaker
soloing *Freerider*
(5.12d)

© Dustin Moore

The second crux and the hardest of the route to my amazement passes without drama. Now though, pitches that should feel easy hurt
instead. Jumaring burns my biceps. Pulling the rope and racking the
gear raws my skin.

The final crux is an all-out battle. I arrive at the final quarter of the
pitch and realise I won't be able to hold on long enough on the top
section to tend the rope or correct any glitches or snags on the solo
device while I'm free climbing. My arms are too tired for that and my
brain is too tired to think when my body is so sore.

I judge the distance to the anchor and pull a huge loop of slack
through the solo device to match. I look again. Look down at the
large loop of slack. Then pull out an extra two metres of rope just to
be sure I don't short-rope myself. I clip my remaining gear to my last
piece to rid the weight; I won't be needing it for this final section.

Even though I'm already three quarters of the way up the pitch and
760 metres off the ground, I still do that strange thing of checking
my rope is secured to the anchor below me and that I'm still attached
to the rope via the solo device. They are. 'Okay that's good,' I tell
myself.

I run through the possibilities of how the next section will go, all
the time while bridging between two small edges and hanging from
a finger lock.

I start with the worst possibility, a fall while clipping the anchor.
What if I do fall clipping the anchor with all this 'guessed amount'
of slack out? Well, I'll just take a monster fall into the corner, which
is fine. I'm too tired at the moment to be even bothered about that.
I just need to make sure I don't hurt myself in that fall.

**After rationalising the worst outcome, I move on to my
positive thoughts of succeeding with an all-out battle.
I am battered, but sure I can do it.**

I am stronger than the last quarter of this pitch. I can definitely
do it. Now with a monster loop of slack dangling uselessly below my
feet, I switch to fast layback mode and grind my hip up against the
right wall and my body towards the anchor. Left foot smearing on the
face, right foot cammed into the corner, left hand peeling away from
the slopey layback and right hand catching the next layback just

in time. I claw my way to the last hold on the pitch. My daisy chain is already off my harness, already prepared for a speedy clip into the anchor. I grab at it, throw it in the direction of the anchor out to my left and release all points of contact when I see the karabiner wrap itself around the bolt.

My body relaxes and every muscle, muscles I didn't even know existed, cramps and ceases with exhaustion. I slump against the wall, head dropped and only then appreciate the huge amount of air (which my looped rope dangles helplessly in) between myself and my last piece of gear.

From here there are five pitches remaining, each in turn getting easier, but only slightly. As I get more tired they each prove to be as much of a battle as that final crux.

I scramble the final ten metres, reaching safety, and collapse to a heap in a moment of catharsis. 'Mike', my solo device, still lies silent by my waist. I am alone, in the blazing midday sun, twenty hours and six minutes after starting.

━ ▪ ━

MARGO HAYES

RECONSTRUCTION

Most of my climbing trips begin with an objective, and my trip to Smith Rock, Oregon State Park, was no different.

I wanted to clip the chains on *Scarface*, the first ever 5.14 equipped and climbed by an American, Scott Franklin.

After trying the route on my first day, I began to have doubts. The tendons in my fingers were sore, and fear of hurting myself started to creep into my thoughts. I was negatively projecting into the future. The next morning, after much deliberation, I decided to walk away from *Scarface* and attempt a few other Smith Rock classics. I had lost my enthusiasm, and a sadness that I couldn't quite identify settled inside me. As I sat at the Aggro Gully sector, I realised that the sadness I was feeling was the result of holding myself back from my goal, my joy. I was creating my own obstacles. I was limiting my potential due to a fear of the future, of what could happen. In my heart, I knew that I could climb *Scarface*. I also recognised that by living in fear of possibly injuring myself on a mono or a small pocket, I was not living in the present.

In the end, I made the conscious decision to pour my effort into my goal, no matter the possible, yet improbable consequences. I returned to the route with a positive outlook. I enjoyed each movement and every attempt. I believed in my ability. A few days later I successfully climbed through the bottom crux for the first time. Once I pulled on to the slightly better holds that followed, I whispered to myself, 'This is it, I don't want to pull on that mono again! Make it happen!'

It wasn't the perfect attempt. It surely wasn't one of those times where it all feels remarkably easy. I made my way up the mid-section of the route, which resembles the bow of a ship, into the second crux. I pushed my doubts aside and made the moves up over the bulge and on to the slab section. I stood there and looked up at the wall, seemingly blank despite the tiny holds and sparse bolts. This section is mentally challenging and I embraced it. I felt free. I enjoyed each moment. I took some time to look across the valley and appreciate

MARGO HAYES + BORN 1998 IN THE USA + HUGELY TALENTED + REPEATED *BAD GIRLS CLUB* (F9A) + JUNIOR WORLD CHAMPION LEAD AND BOULDERING IN 2016 + 2017 FIRST WOMAN TO CLIMB F9A+ – *LA RAMBLA* IN SPAIN

the beauty. As I approached the chains, I felt proud. I had summoned up my courage and prevailed over my inner turmoil. I had broken through my self-imposed impediments.

Scarface gave me confidence in myself and the strength to fight my fears.

■ ▪ ■

Margo Hayes
climbing
Scarface (5.14a)

© Tara Kerzhner

STEVE MC CLURE

STRAWBERRIES

One of the most famous routes in the history of British climbing. It was first climbed by Ron Fawcett in 1980 using pre-placed and pre-clipped protection, but some questioned the ethics.

The quality and difficulty of the route have since become legendary. Jerry Moffatt stepped in to make an early repeat, dishing Fawcett's ascent and causing a public outcry. The route was already on its way to fame. *Strawberries* takes the thin crack splitting the overhanging headwall of the Vector Buttress at Tremadog in North Wales. Way up in the sky and hanging over the road it is visible to every passerby, climber or not. Boasting extreme exposure the line cannot be ignored. It is the symbol of hard climbing.

For me, it's always been there. At ten years old, *Strawberries* had just been climbed, just as I found myself falling in love with climbing. Poring over the headlines and the pictures is my very first memory of the world of extreme rock. They stayed with me. They stayed with everyone from that generation. New routes came along, harder ones, but *Strawberries* remained king. The classic hard challenge with all the right ingredients: perfect rock, masses of exposure, bold but with good gear, hard, technical and at one of the UK's finest crags.

I came and went to Tremadog many times, always with *Strawberries* towering above. We'd stare up in awe and even struggle up the routes skirting the edge of the buttress. *Void* and *Cream* were a battle – just how hard could *Strawberries* be? Slowly my ability increased, but only at the same pace as the route gathered its fearsome reputation. It remained one step ahead, maybe more than one step.

Stefan Glowacz made the first on-sight back in 1987. Despite being world champion his ascent was still ahead of its time and it took another twenty-four years for the next repeat in this style from Jorg Verhoeven. The on-sight was the challenge. Many tried, all the UK's top climbers, but all came away empty-handed, each adding to a reputation growing out of control. I waited for the right time, saving it for an on-sight effort, waiting for everything to fall perfectly

STEVE MCCLURE + BORN 1970 IN THE UK + ONE OF THE BEST ROCK CLIMBERS IN THE WORLD + CLIMBED THE HARDEST SPORT ROUTE IN THE UK – *RAINMAN* (F9B) + CLIMBED NUMEROUS NEW F9A ROUTES AND ON-SIGHTED MANY F8B+ ROUTES

into place. I kept waiting, putting it off, avoiding it, full of excuses. In reality, I was scared of it. The route was too big for me.

But suddenly, I crossed a threshold and realised my time was running out. I watched as years went by without even getting a chance: too wet, too much work, too injured. I didn't even get to the cliff! I just wanted to do it, even if I fell on-sight. What did it really matter compared to never trying? To leave *Strawberries* untried would be my greatest failure.

A diary slot appeared and a great partner in Rab Carrington. Butterflies arrived before even committing and then suddenly there I was, staring up from the road as I had done so many times before. It was dry and clean and there was chalk on it. The air was clear and a light breeze drifted over the cliff. I felt rested.

My chance was now! There could be no waiting. And so I gave in to it and boarded the conveyer belt of preparation, drifted into position, sorted the belay, racked up, psyched up.

I was there now, no backing out. The fear overwhelmed me. The reputation of the route made my mouth dry and my body shake. I wasn't scared of falling, or of failing. I was just scared of the route.

Calm down. Deep breaths. Let's get a grip. They say climbing is all in the mind. Maybe it is.

I was out of control; like running too fast down a steep rocky hill about to fall over flat on my face. I needed to stop and then start again at the right pace, take each step at a time. It was gonna be hard, I knew that, of course, but I needed to be ready, not throwing myself headlong into battle without any weapons. E7 6b, or French 7c, maybe 7c+ placing protection. Hard, but I'd on-sighted over 800 at 8a or above. So chances were good. But if I did fall, so what? I'd be able to do it next go, guaranteed. Still a childhood dream. It wouldn't matter either way. Who cared? No one, except me. My reputation wouldn't be shattered and anyway who would even know? It was just me versus the route, all I had to do was give it my best shot.

Calmer now. Some planning. Keep it simple. I knew the line, it's obvious. I knew where the hard bits were, obvious too. I could see a rest before the crux and good protection. What protection? Cams, small to medium, maybe a few wires. Slim down the rack, fast and light, simple and easy. With good gear I could go to the top without even thinking of more; the fall zone is clean. Knowing this was crucial. It would be safe. I could climb to the max. I'd aim for the rest, that would be my first target. I'd place the gear, assess, absorb the holds, then go flat out.

In the end, it wouldn't matter how I would do. I just needed to give it my best, that's all I could do. I was ready.

Steve McClure
on-sighting
Strawberries
(E7 6b)

© Tim Glasby

PAUL REEVE

CRY FREEDOM

It's May and the days are relentlessly running out for this part of the Malham season. Working full time and continuously balancing everything else in life. Time has become an obsession for me.

After years of injury, I have finally got fit enough to climb to the finishing boulder crux of *Cry Freedom* (F8c) without being tired. In my own mind, this means climbing 8b to a poor shake-out. From then on, I proceed time and again to throw myself at the last three moves. Tick, Tick, Tick. Slowly, but surely, I am feeling more and more confident I could do the route. Then I slip and fall one metre from the ledge at the base of the cliff and tear a back muscle.

Facing the prospect of sitting around all day, I roll my back again and again on my stainless steel flask to relieve the pain. I spend an hour trying to warm up, and then in frustration, I make the stupid decision of tying into a top rope on the route. In the light rain, conditions are excellent (the cliff is so steep rain never hits it) and I find myself at the top crux having climbed the route with no expectation. Instead of completing the crux on top rope, I force myself to jump off so as not to put a jinx on a true redpoint ascent that may never happen.

Another week passes before I can go back, then a cold comes on – man flu! Instead of resting, I go up on the Sunday and throw myself off the top of the route again and a second time for luck. Another bigger mistake. For the next three weeks, I just feel terrible. Tired and lifeless. Sitting at work, meeting after meeting, all I can do is think about the reasons why I couldn't or wouldn't do this route.

June comes along, game over according to normal rules. However, one thing about the two-hour journey from Sheffield to Malham is the infamous banter and discussion. The message is clear: stick with it, you're too close to stop now.

My allocated annual leave has run out, so I make the decision to commit to going up after work for a late evening redpoint. Scratching around for a belayer, no one from Sheffield is interested in driving two and a half hours through bumper-to-bumper rush hour traffic.

PAUL REEVE + BORN 1962 + FIRST F8C AT THE AGE OF FIFTY + RIDICULOUS MOTIVATION, WHEN HE DID HIS FIRST 8B+ HE HAD BEEN IN MEETINGS ALL DAY, FINISHED AT 5 P.M., DROVE THREE AND A HALF HOURS, REDPOINTED *MECCA* AND DROVE BACK FOR MEETINGS THE NEXT MORNING + LOVES RUNNING + DID THE BOB GRAHAM ROUND (SIXTY-SIX MILES, OVER 8,000 METRES OF ASCENT), IN TWENTY-THREE HOURS AND TWENTY-SIX MINUTES HOURS (THE CHALLENGE IS TO DO IT IN UNDER TWENTY-FOUR HOURS)

Paul Reeve
climbing
Cry Freedom
(F8c)

© Keith Sharples

Stressful! Fortunately, I'm able to hook up with a few locals still climbing after work. So after three desperate evenings in those 'classic' windless, warm, humid and midgey Malham evenings, I am still falling off the last move. It is all too much; I am feeling physically tired. Mentally, my confidence, well, it has gone. So that coming weekend, I commit to my last trip up for that year. Going through the motions, I drive to Malham with my belayer, Seb, who is good enough to go up with me. Well, who knows? One last chance before the season is over.

Saturday is overcast, dry and warm, but there is a wind blowing. Having arrived, I can feel it dropping off and getting warmer; yet another excuse getting ready for failure. After warming up, I tie in and race to the top of the route, only to throw myself off the finishing crux yet again. This is it, I'm finished. Relief in a way, another season has escaped me. I'm now staring down the barrel of the gun; my fifty-first birthday is three months away. I haven't got what it takes and I can't find it; just accept it and move on. So I'm hanging there at the top of the route when I look down and see Steve Dunning (who is also trying the route) turning up at the crag to climb. I imagine for some reason he feels pity for me as he looks up with a smile. I also sense the self-confidence that Steve has around himself, knowing that he is going to do what I can't. I'm finished for the day. But in that moment something happens that changes the negative thought pattern, but I don't know it. I know I have been fighting injury, illness and conditions for weeks. I know I'm good at dealing with adversity, but something has been missing. Seb lets me down; I untie. He redpoints on his route and we have a bit of brutal banter. I tell him I'm going to walk round the top of the crag. At this point, I'm totally consumed in my own head, deep inside digging and scratching around for something, but who knows what? But, I do know my body is signalling it's tired, and realistically I don't have another redpoint in me. I arrive at the top of the steps and walk over to the Harry Potter Campsite at the top of Malham. It is a stunning panorama looking out across the English countryside. I have it all to myself. I sit down and I'm lost in thought, deep thought.

All I remember is visualising the point of my failure again and again, but I daydream to the point where I suddenly feel myself mentally doing the crux and the feeling of subsequent elation. I get up and go down the steps. I have nothing to lose, no expectation and I feel in a good mood.

Looking back, I can only remember tying in and then waking up midway through the final crux at the top of the route. My right hand has hold of the sloper which I can never reach well enough to crimp. I'm not dropping it. Bam! The reality of the situation hits me. The adrenaline kicks in, I'm about to panic, time slows down. In the intensity of the moment, I find myself looking at my whole body. My left foot is in a heel-and-toe lock, the left hand is in the thin undercut. My brain is calmly sending out the thoughts required to break the lock by removing the heel and toe to a bunched-up smear that normally pushes me off; the right hand is still holding. I go again with my right hand. One more move to relative safety. I've not dropped it. I hold it together for one more sequence and it's done!

For me, it's a million-dollar moment that's worth more than all that plastic crap you can buy with your debit card. Twenty minutes later you are wondering what's next.

Looking back, I realise now I had let all the negatives become the norm. On reflection, that was a bad mistake and that nearly cost me my lucky day.

BARBARA ZANGERL

Babsi Zangerl
climbing
Bellavista (F8c)

© Thomas Senf

BELLAVISTA

The reason I decided to try *Bellavista* (F8c on the huge face of Cima Ovest di Lavaredo) was that I wanted to gain experience climbing in the Alps, where I would have to handle my fear on a really exposed wall, making it hard to just concentrate on the climbing.

I would also at the same time need to learn to trust pitons, bad gear and how to climb on loose rock where you dare not pull too hard to reach the next hold.

Sometimes the quality of the rock meant that climbing felt more like pushing than pulling, especially on the easy pitches of *Bellavista*. On the first days, the insecure feeling was intense and I didn't trust any holds. Sometimes I was dreaming of the solid rock in Rätikon (Switzerland), as this is the rock quality I normally feel comfortable with. I was questioning myself: why am I spending so much time on a hard route on this always-wet north face? But this challenge was different and this was why this route was so interesting to me. At the same time, it was hard to keep up my motivation.

In the summer 2014, when Jacopo and I first climbed up to the roof where the crux pitches are, we got stopped several times by the challenge of the 'easy' lower pitches. We got stressed out holding on to wet, slimy holds never knowing whether we would slip off or not. Sometimes a fall was not really an option. We were sure there would be no chance to climb the hard sequences in these conditions. After those attempts I thought okay, maybe that's the deal and we just have to get used to it.

Jacopo was trying *Pan Aroma* at the same time I was trying *Bella-vista*. *Pan Aroma* shares the first pitches to the roof and at the roof *Pan Aroma* turns right and *Bellavista* goes left. The roof of the West Cime, called one of the biggest climbable roofs in the Alps, is what makes *Bellavista* and *Pan Aroma* so special. *Pan Aroma* is also an Alex Huber testpiece and harder than *Bellavista* with huge run-outs. Hats off to Alex who did the first ascents of these incredible routes.

After a few days we both felt familiar with our routes, and our first

BARBARA 'BABSI' ZANGERL+ BORN 1988 + FIRST WOMAN TO CLIMB A FONT 8B BOULDER – *PURA VIDA* IN MAGIC WOOD + REPEATED HARD MULTI-PITCH CLIMBS LIKE *SILBERGEIER* F8B+ AND SCARY TRAD ROUTES SUCH AS *PRINZIP HOFFNUNG* F8B/+ (E9/10)

impressions eased. But the weather was not on our side and I was too weak to climb the route in these conditions. It turned out to be a real trial of patience over two months, climbing in dense fog without seeing each other and spending time on the roof drying up holds with hankies. Apart from that, we always felt satisfied and optimistic that everything would turn out great. Like the time together in Jacopo's old messy car and in our little food tent, cooking in the rain and drinking beer at the Auronzo hut. Maybe that is not the summer vacation people dream of, but it was a really intense experience that taught us a little more about ourselves.

One year later, I went back to *Bellavista* together with Christian Winklmair who is known as Pinky. Everything was different from what I had expected. The conditions were much better than on every single day the year before and after spending some time practising the crux I decided to give the route a ground-up try the following day.

I didn't expect to send the route and I didn't take it too seriously because we both knew that we had to work the day after.

We also knew that it would take us too long to climb the remaining twenty-four pitches to the summit so we got up around eight and started climbing around half past nine. I felt really self-confident and less scared while leading all the pitches up to the hardest.

On the crux pitch, I had a big fight against my pumped forearms. When I reached the belay without falling I was really happy, but the real adventure had only just started. We left our haulbag with all the heavy stuff and at seven o'clock in the evening after some spicy pitches we finally reached the big ledge where *Bellavista* meets the classic *Cassin* route. We had fourteen more pitches to climb following the *Cassin* route. We decided to swing leads which made us faster, but regardless of that, after a few pitches it was totally dark. We kept on climbing with our head torches for nine more pitches to the top. It was quite hard to find the few single pitons and also the belays. Sometimes we just built our own belays and we muddled along the way up to the top and reached the summit at two o'clock in the morning in the bright shining moonlight. This was for sure one of my most intense and incredible climbing days ever.

MICH KEMETER

Mich Kemeter
highlining
between two hot
air balloons

© Alex Buisse

HIGHLINE IN THE SKY

Sharing a deep bond with the earth means quite a lot to me. Being connected with nature gives me this spiritual feeling of inner balance, guiding my thoughts and dreams.

One night I had this fantastic dream about a highline in the sky. It was a split second of a dream, but when it came true it lasted for minutes of absolute joy and happiness. When I began to actually live out that dream there were many thoughts, fear and unknown feelings. I had to find a way for real to embrace the joy and happiness I experienced during this walk in the air in my dream.

I walked many highlines free solo in the past – world record lines above water, the ground and at many heights. Many free-solo routes and solo-BASE climbs were part of an adventure that was always created in my own world first, in my mind. Mastering the complex movements and special knowledge required a few years of intensive training, pushing my limits and learning. Many close friends died along this path. I was constantly asking myself why am I still alive, why I am able to do this kind of 'art' – while having a big smile on my face doing it? The answer is easy:

It's the focus. The intense focus on being in the 'NOW', not in the past or the future ...

One day, apparently my birthday, I knew I wanted to do it – the walk in the air. After sorting out the logistics my highline was finally connected between two hot air balloons.

The crew was ready for take-off, but we were worried about strong winds. Was it a sign? Yes. But we took off anyway.

I struggled with some new feelings. First, I had never been in a hot air balloon before. Second, I had never fallen off a highline unleashed.

MICH KEMETER + BORN 1988 + PROFESSIONAL SLACKLINER, CLIMBER AND BASE JUMPER + MANY SLACKLINE WORLD RECORDS + SPORT CLIMBS UP TO F8C+ + CLIMBS SOLO-BASE WHICH IS SOLOING WITH A PARACHUTE

So I was pretty nervous during the actual take-off, but I was mentally prepared. It almost felt like I'd done it before, like a movie I had already seen. We didn't have enough time and gas for a long session. I also thought that it wasn't necessary to bring a harness and a leash to walk this magic line safely, that I would be confident walking it only with my BASE rig on my back. A leash would have made the situation and the very first step so much easier though. It's always a challenge to walk a line on the first go, without knowing how much tension is on it and how much strength it requires. So this was the crux this time: THE FIRST STEP. Usually, I visualise the last step before I even attempt the first one and I have a nice journey. But then, at this exposed sunset line, 1,000 metres above ground (El Cap height), I had a mind game running. This movie was a new one indeed. Time and gas were running out; we couldn't stay in the air much longer. My mind was calculating: what happens if I fall? Will I survive? Will I black out due to the mental pressure, for no reason? All of these thoughts made it up with me, so far above the ground. I wished I had taken the harness and safety leash with me so I would have a second chance, but my gear was not there. Just my thoughts and my mental 'strength'. I thought, 'Now is the moment to prove myself without a second chance.' I did the first step and realised that my weight pulled the hot air balloons together. While I was taking the second, I was out in space. My mind was clear again; everything that bothered me before was gone.

I was breathing, focusing and taking another step forward. I felt amazingly at ease.

My focus point was on the other balloon, as there was still quite a lot of wind. Suddenly I fell, but I caught the line and returned to the basket as fast as I could. My mind was still not relaxed enough. All my negative thoughts came flooding into my mind again, but I tried to stay focused in the 'NOW'. I used a breathing technique to calm down until they told me I only had thirty seconds left before they had to cut the line. At this moment, I felt the inner tension more than ever, quite a new experience for me. I also knew I would probably feel that way again and again over the next few seconds and I would have to find a way to deal with it. I managed to do the first step, but after the second I fell off again. Two days later, I walked the whole line five times. I was ready for it then. Well, sometimes you just have to have an idea about what is going to happen before you play hard.

LEO HOULDING

Leo Houlding
climbing
Dinosaur's Spine

© Alastair Lee

THE DINOSAUR'S SPINE, NORTH-EAST RIDGE OF

ULVETANNA

Ulvetanna, the wolf's fang in Norwegian, is the jewel in the crown of the Fenriskjeften (the jaw of the Fenris wolf), a spectacular group of granite spires in Queen Maud Land, Eastern Antarctica. It is the most technically demanding peak on the harshest continent.

It looks like a mountain a child would draw, a prodigious granite fang protruding from the endless white desert of the Antarctic ice cap, steep on all sides with no easy way to the top.

The gargantuan north-east ridge is the mountain's most striking feature. Cutting a line between light and shade, a knife-edge ridge sits between two huge vertical walls; rising for over a mile of continuous, serious rock climbing it is comparable in perfection to any line on any cliff or peak anywhere.

I first became aware of these fantasy mountains shortly after I finished school when I was given a copy of Ivar Tollefsen's inspirational book of the expedition he led that discovered this mythical range so remote it lay hidden from the world until as late as 1994.

Upon first glance I thought to myself, 'One day, I'm going to climb that mountain.'

Back then, I had never climbed a big wall, had no expedition experience and was just beginning to flirt with sponsorship. I had no idea quite how challenging or expensive it would be simply to reach the base of the peak, never mind the summit.

A wall-style ascent of El Capitan at over 25 °C in California's glorious conditions is committing, exposed and seriously strenuous. Just existing in a remote polar base camp at -25 °C is intimidating, exhausting and requires constant diligence to stay abreast of the situation.

LEO HOULDING + BORN 1980 IN THE UK + KNOWN FOR HARD BOLD TRAD + FIRST ASCENTS OF *TRAUMA* (E8 7A) & *RARE LICHEN* (E9 6C) + FREE CLIMBED BIG WALLS SUCH AS *EL NINO* AND *FREERIDER* ON EL CAP + OPENED *THE PROPHET* (E9 7A) + NOW SPECIALISING IN ASCENTS IN REMOTE AREAS LIKE MOUNT ASGARD ON BAFFIN ISLAND, CERRO AUTANA IN VENEZUELA OR ULVETANNA IN ANTARCTICA

Combining these two hardships, big-wall climbing in Antarctica really is a very serious undertaking requiring a wealth of experience, knowledge, skill and resilience. Raising the six-figure finance for such a mission is an equal challenge in itself.

It took me fifteen years, but finally in December 2012 my wildest dream came true and with a six-man, tried and tested crew of some of my closest friends we stood awestruck beneath the mighty north-east ridge of Ulvetanna contemplating the enormity and magnificence of our ambition.

I have always been a free climber, but in my heart I knew that temperatures would almost certainly dictate the use of aid to make the first ascent of Ulvetanna's north-east ridge. However, conditions were unexpectedly kind early in the ascent and to our great surprise we were able to free climb the first 1,200 metres of the route with many incredible pitches of stern climbing freed on-sight or first redpoint after inspection and cleaning. Eventually our free-climbing efforts were indeed defeated, ironically on what would've been a relatively straightforward pitch, but impossible to climb without gloves or aid in -25 °C.

Of all the climbing I've ever done, the central section of the north-east ridge stands out. A truly knife-edge ridge, about forty-five degrees in angle, 250 metres in length, no more than one metre wide, with vertical walls that fall away for at least 500 metres on both sides and set high above the otherworldly landscape of the Antarctica plateau. It is the most uniquely perfect piece of rock architecture I have encountered. We called it the *Dinosaur's Spine*.

Exposure is something that has always appealed to me about climbing. Being out on a limb, putting yourself on the line, presenting yourself in harm's way and being completely reliant upon yourself to deal with the situation.

Standing below the *Dinosaur's Spine* on the Col of False Hope with my best mate Jason Pickles looking up along that beautifully aesthetic, unclimbed line, summoning the courage to quest up into the void was one of the highlights of my life as a climber.

Though the climbing looked pretty easy, the rock was crumbly and utterly devoid of cracks, and hence protection, for almost its entirety. Exposed beyond words. Never before touched by human hands.

The shady side of the ridge was fifteen degrees colder than the already freezing sunny side. I climbed it without great difficulty, but with frozen hands in ever-increasing danger for a full rope length without placing a single piece of gear until the rope went tight. At that point, I sat down on the ridge and hand drilled two 8-millimetre bolts to make a belay. I brought up Jas and then repeated for three almost identical pitches.

Towards the end of the final pitch the ridge got steeper. It was no longer possible to simply pad up. I had to start finding finger and footholds amongst the crumbly crystals of the granite. The rope fell virtually clean for a full pitch. As I inched upwards some surface crust crumbled and my foot skated.

In that split second, I felt more exposed than at any time before or since – truly out there in every way.

But the skate was not entirely unexpected; I knew the rock was crusty and was practising old school, three-points-of-contact technique. I finished the sequence unperturbed, but those easy moves were definitely some of the most memorable of my climbing life.

On top of the ridge we reached a fantastic, harness-off ledge perched directly below the towering, vertical headwall. A long way from home and still very far from our distant goal. For the first time on the expedition, it felt like we may actually achieve our wildest dream and reach Ulvetanna's most elusive summit.

After twenty years searching for the next great epic, I have found that the most fulfilling climbing experiences are those that bring you the closest to the edge, but without stumbling over it. The greatest successes are those snatched from the jaws of defeat.

The harder you try, the more complications and challenges you face. The closer you push towards the point of disaster, but crucially without reaching it, but ending up on top and ultimately safely back at the bottom are the most powerful and memorable ascents.

Ulvetanna was a life-long dream. The reality did not disappoint.

Leo Houlding
climbing
Dinosaur's Spine

© Alastair Lee

MAYAN SMITH-GOBAT

Mayan
Smith-Gobat
climbing *Riders
on the Storm*

© Thomas Senf

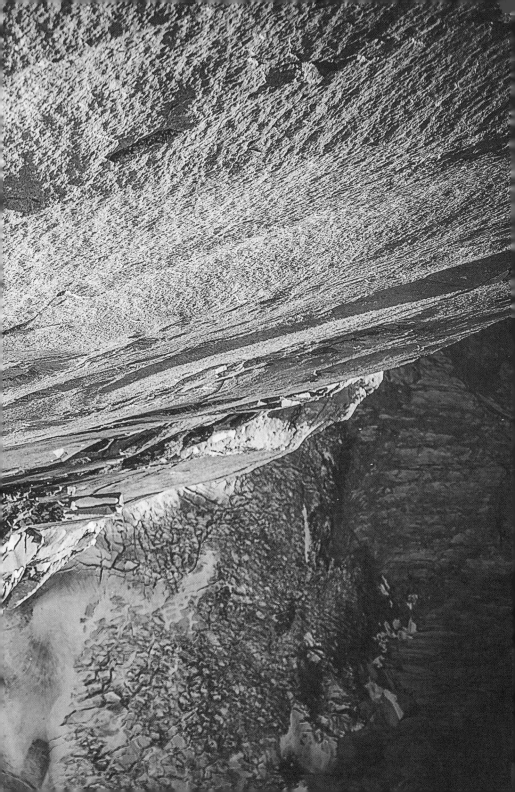

RIDERS ON THE STORM

Frozen snow crunched under my crampons and the heavy haulbag cut into my shoulders as I trudged across the glacier in the soft early morning sunlight. Every few steps I glanced up, not able to keep my eyes off the steep wall towering above us.

An impossibly steep, blank monolith of granite which appeared to keep growing with every step we took, *Riders on the Storm* has always stood out in climbing history, a route beyond its time. The climbing legends Wolfgang Güllich, Kurt Albert, Bernd Arnold, Norbert Bätz and Peter Dittrich made the first ascent over twenty-five years ago now. This was before I had begun climbing and when these remote granite spires in Patagonia were relatively untouched by climbers.

In mid-2016, when Ines Papert suggested trying to free climb *Riders on the Storm* I was simultaneously filled with boundless excitement, fear and intimidation. This route had turned away so many of the world's best climbers and alpinists. 'Could Ines and I really even have a chance on this incredible route?' was the question which kept running through my mind. I felt inadequately prepared, but as Ines and I discussed the idea in more detail I realised that where I lacked skills, Ines was very experienced. We balanced each other perfectly, and I soon realised that saying 'no' was never really an option. I love stepping outside of my comfort zone and trying to find where my boundaries are. To progress, I have often forced myself to step into a realm that I perceived as impossible for me.

Six months later, as Ines and I slowly worked our way up the varied features of this huge vertical wall, I regularly felt very small and entirely out of my depth. Before heading down to Patagonia, I believed that I would be reasonably well prepared through spending years climbing on the thousand-metre walls in Yosemite. But now that I saw Torre Central towering above me and experienced the incredible power of nature here. El Capitan seemed like sport climbing in comparison.

After almost three weeks fighting our way up the wall, Ines and I were standing below the last hard pitches of the route. Totally

MAYAN SMITH-GOBAT + BORN 1979 + HALF KIWI AND HALF GERMAN CLIMBER + EXPLORING CRAGS ALL OVER THE WORLD FROM CHINA TO PATAGONIA + REPEATED WOLFGANG GÜLLICH'S *PUNKS IN THE GYM* (F8b+) IN AUSTRALIA + FREE CLIMBED THE *SALATHÉ WALL* IN 2011 ON EL CAP IN CALIFORNIA + FEMALE SPEED RECORD ON *THE NOSE*

exhausted from over 1,000 metres of climbing in constant cold, jumaring nearly 600 metres every day and only having the occasional day off the wall, our bodies were falling apart, yet only sixty metres separated us from the mellower ground to the summit. However, these sixty metres were one of the biggest challenges, if we still hoped to free climb *Riders on the Storm* – a drastically overhanging finger crack which had never had a free ascent.

'TO PROGRESS, I HAVE OFTEN FORCED MYSELF TO STEP INTO A REALM THAT I PERCEIVED AS IMPOSSIBLE FOR ME ... '

MAYAN
SMITH-GOBAT

W1500M

Ines and I spent a day working out the moves. Thin sharp finger locks, small crimpers and powerful sequences made for an incredible sustained thirty-metre pitch. On our last attempt that day, both Ines and I came close, but both fell on a large dynamic throw into an upside-down finger lock. Frozen to the bone, with bleeding fingers and muscles screaming at us, we rappelled over 600 metres back down to the portaledges, attempting to rest and refuel our bodies as best we could. A weather update showed that there was only one more day of good weather before a large storm was predicted. This was our chance for the summit and we knew that we would have to go to the top, then take our ropes down whether the crux pitch went free or not.

Waking at 2 a.m. after a restless night's sleep, I slowly patched the countless holes in my fingers back together with glue and tape. Nearly every single tip was bleeding, deeply cracked and swollen to nearly twice the size. Forcing some breakfast down, I threw some bars into my pocket and crept out into the bitterly cold night.

Snapping my jumars on to the frozen rope, I started the long commute to our high point – a brutal 600 metres and almost two hours of free-hanging jugging. However, soon the monotonous movement allowed me to slip into a dreamlike state. As the sky brightened a lone condor circled effortlessly past, 'at one' with the constant winds that carried him upward. His dark eyes stared straight through me as though questioning my clumsiness, my separation from the world of wind and air, from the wild freedom that he enjoyed. In that moment, joy and wonder flooded my entire being. I forgot all the pain and exhaustion, my movements becoming effortless. In that moment I was at peace, dangling off a tiny rope 1,500 metres above the glacier – a guest with the rare privilege to exist in this beautiful and unforgiving place. Ines and I reached the top of our fixed lines at 6 a.m., just as the fireball of the sun rose over darkened plains. It was a perfect cloudless morning – the only one we experienced in those six weeks. Absorbing the first golden rays I focused my entire being on that sensation of inner quiet as I pulled on my rock shoes and prepared to climb. We only had time for one attempt before the wall became a running waterfall.

I knew that it was now or never, but as I peeled off my thick down jacket and gloves I let go of any pressures or expectations to send.

I sucked in a deep breath of icy air and within seconds, my fingers and toes lost all sensation. Feeling nothing, I simply had to give every movement everything I had and trust that my hands and feet would hold. My focus narrowed: blocking out everything else and believing in myself entirely. I twisted my hands into the narrow opening and my skin ripped open in new places. Yet, I didn't feel a thing, I simply buried my fingers deeper; the small patches of blood on the stone turned to rivulets.

'*Komm schon, gib alles!*' (Give it everything!) Ines shouted up in German, her energy feeding into mine. With every remnant of strength left in my exhausted body, I lunged toward a slight widening far above me. To my surprise, my numb hand landed perfectly, wedged into the thin crack without even feeling the dimensions of the rock.

'I did it!' My mind screamed instantly followed by the thought 'Now don't blow it!' I tried to calm my breathing, pushing these thoughts away. My limbs felt heavy, my hands were dripping with blood and I could feel the pump building in my forearms. Pulling on all of my knowledge from over twenty years of climbing, I moved through the next twelve metres with slow control and precision. Elation swelled inside me like a wave as I reached around the final lip and felt warm, dry rock. I heaved my body on to a ledge. Finally, I could let go. I gave an ecstatic cry!

Executing this pitch at the top of the 1,300-metre Torre Central had required me to draw on every single piece of skill and knowledge I had gathered throughout my entire life.

From growing up amongst the New Zealand Alps, to spending years bouldering on the powerful holdless features of Castle Hill, from countless redpoint attempts on *Punks in the Gym*, learning to control my mental space, to the months learning to crack climb on the headwall of the *Salathé*.

MAYAN
SMITH-GOBAT

In that instant, it felt as though all those experiences had all culminated in that moment.

'ENTIRELY BELIEVE IN YOURSELF!'

It enabled me to add a small piece to the history of *Riders on the Storm*. Twenty-five years had passed since the Germans had first aided this crack and I had just free climbed it. Was this real? The crisp air sparkled brighter as I gazed out over the endless plains. For an instant, I felt as if I shared the condor's freedom. My mind soared, limitless space and light dropping away beneath my feet.

LESSON

LESSON

LESSON

LESSON

LESSON